LEARN TO PAINT WITH
OILS, ACRYLICS
AND GOUACHE

with 25 step-by-step painting projects

• Learn to paint people,
animals, landscapes,
seascapes, still lifes,
buildings and flowers
through taught examples

• All the traditional and
modern oil, acrylic and
gouache techniques you
need to know in one
easy-to-follow volume

IAN SIDAWAY

southwater

This edition is published by Southwater

Southwater is an imprint of Anness Publishing Ltd
Hermes House, 88–89 Blackfriars Road, London SE1 8HA
tel. 020 7401 2077; fax 020 7633 9499
www.southwaterbooks.com; info@anness.com

© Anness Publishing Ltd 2006

UK agent: The Manning Partnership Ltd
6 The Old Dairy, Melcombe Road, Bath BA2 3LR
tel. 01225 478444; fax 01225 478440
sales@manning-partnership.co.uk

UK distributor: Grantham Book Services Ltd
Isaac Newton Way, Alma Park Industrial Estate
Grantham, Lincs NG31 9SD
tel. 01476 541080; fax 01476 541061
orders@gbs.tbs-ltd.co.uk

North American agent/distributor: National Book Network
4501 Forbes Boulevard, Suite 200, Lanham, MD 20706
tel. 301 459 3366; fax 301 429 5746; www.nbnbooks.com

Australian agent/distributor: Pan Macmillan Australia
Level 18, St Martins Tower, 31 Market St, Sydney, NSW 2000
tel. 1300 135 113; fax 1300 135 103;
customer.service@macmillan.com.au

New Zealand agent/distributor: David Bateman Ltd
30 Tarndale Grove, Off Bush Road, Albany, Auckland
tel. (09) 415 7664; fax (09) 415 8892

Previously published as part of a larger volume,
The Practical Encyclopedia of Acrylics, Oils and Gouache

Publisher: Joanna Lorenz
Editorial Director: Helen Sudell
Editors: Sarah Hoggett and Elizabeth Woodland
Photographers: George Taylor
Designer: Nigel Partridge
Cover Designer: Nigel Partridge
Project Contributors: Martin Decent, Paul Dyson, Timothy Easton,
Abigail Edgar, Wendy Jelbert, John Raynes, Ian Sidaway
Production Controller: Claire Rae

1 3 5 7 9 10 8 6 4 2

Acknowledgements
The publishers are grateful to the staff at Paintworks,
99–101 Kingsland Road, London E2 8AG for the generous
loan of materials and equipment.

Special thanks to the following artists for their
demonstrations and step-by-step projects:
Martin Decent: pages 54–9, 66–71, 80–5, 124–9.
Paul Dyson: pages 14–17, 32–7.
Timothy Easton: pages 18–23, 60–5, 86–91, 100–5.
Abigail Edgar: pages 50–3, 112–17, 132–7, 144–9.
Wendy Jelbert: pages 8–13, 38–43, 74–9, 118–23.
John Raynes: pages 124–9, 44–7, 106–111, 150–5.
Ian Sidaway: pages 92–7, 138–43.

Thanks to the following for their kind permission
to reproduce copyright photographs and paintings:
Keith Adams: page 44 (top). Martin Decent: pages 7 (top),
30, 49 (top), 73 (top), 100, 131 (bottom).
Timothy Easton: pages 6, 7 (bottom), 31 (both), 48, 49 (bottom),
72, 73 (bottom), 101 (both), 130, 131 (top).

Contents

Introduction

Acrylics, oils and gouache are three very different painting media. Oil paints have an unjustified reputation for being difficult to use. One reason for this may be that we tend to think of oils as being a medium for 'real' artists – for people who have been professionally trained and know what they're doing. Oil painting is something that many of us feel we might aspire to at some stage in the future, when we've cut our teeth on something easier and technically less demanding.

Once you know how the paint handles, however, and have mastered a few basic techniques, you will quickly discover what a joy it is to work with. There is nothing quite like the tactile feeling of smoothing thick, buttery oil paint onto canvas – but you can also use it in a dilute form to create thin, transparent washes of almost infinite subtlety. Unlike watercolour, which has an unnerving tendency to dribble and pool and run into areas where you don't want it to go, oil paint stays where you put it. It also looks exactly the same colour when it is wet and dry, so there is no need to make any allowance for colour shifts when painting. And, most importantly, the long drying time means that you can manipulate the paint on the canvas, or even rework areas of your painting, far more readily than you can with a quick-drying medium.

Acrylics, on the other hand, are often perceived as being at the other end of the scale from oils. First introduced in the 1950s they were, for many years, derided by 'serious' artists as second-rate materials suitable only for illustrators and graphic designers (although why there should be such a distinction between 'fine artists' and illustrators is hard to understand). But instead of turning up our noses, we should learn to celebrate the unique characteristics of acrylics. They really are incredibly versatile: like gouache, you can dilute them and apply them as thin washes; like oil paints, you can use them straight from the tube to create thick, impasto applications in which every stroke of the brush or painting knife can be seen. With acrylics, it seems, you really do get the best of both worlds.

Gouache is sometimes seen as little more than the 'poor relation' of watercolour, as both are water based and the techniques are virtually identical.

Café scene ▼
The artist has used strong blocks of colour to create a wonderful tonal balance in this busy street scene.

Some purists lament the fact that, because the paint is opaque, a painting in gouache can never achieve the translucency and transparency of a watercolour painting. But this belies the fact that gouache is a medium in its own right, with its own special qualities. The inclusion of precipitated chalk in the manufacturing process is what gives gouache its opaque, slightly chalky, matt finish.

This book contains 25 step-by-step projects on all the most popular painting subjects – landscapes, flowers and leaves, still lifes, animals and birds, buildings and people. Here you will find something to suit all tastes, from a beautiful study of irises growing in the wild to a charming painting of a sleeping cat, from an almost deserted beach with sunlight sparkling on the sea to a busy café scene full of people and life. These lively and inspirational works by contemporary artists will provide you with a constant source of inspiration and practical information on how to tackle these subjects.

The projects have been specially commissioned from leading professional artists in order to show you a range of styles and approaches. All the artists featured in this book have built up a wealth of experience over many years of study, which they share here with you in the hope that you will gain as much pleasure and enjoyment from painting in oils, acrylics and gouache as they have experienced. Study them carefully, and learn from the tips and techniques suggested. With time and practice, you will soon be creating works of art that you can be proud to display to your friends and family.

This is not a fool-proof recipe book. As with any creative endeavour, there are no short-cuts: if you want to learn new skills or improve existing ones, the only way to do it is to practise – and then practise some more. However, this volume is an invaluable source book of techniques and approaches to painting that will stand you in good stead for many years to come.

Stormy sky ▲
Here the artist has used complementary colours – the different tones of purple in the buildings against the yellow and blue sky – to create a dusky, dramatic atmosphere.

Tulips in glass vase ▶
This project brings together soft blends of warm and cool colours to create a delightful painting that captures the effect of diffused and reflected light.

Painting flowers and leaves

From tiny meadow flowers growing in the wild to hot-house exotics such as orchids, flowers and leaves are an infinitely appealing subject to paint. The approaches to painting them are equally varied. If it's the subtle coloration of the blooms and foliage that appeals to you, or a particular species of flower, you might choose to concentrate on a single leaf or flower – or even to close in on one or two petals so that your work becomes semi-abstract. Bouquets of cut flowers allow you to explore a number of different blooms in the same arrangement. Alternatively, you might want to paint a floral landscape – a field full of poppies or lavender, perhaps.

Whatever approach you take and whatever medium you are working in, start with the overall shape. Make studies in your sketchbook, looking at how the petals and leaves overlap, where the flower head sits in relation to the stalk, the size and shape of the leaves and so

on. The better you understand the structure, the better your painting will be.

Colour is undoubtedly one of the main reasons for painting flowers; the rich golds and russets of autumn leaves are stunning. If you are painting in oils or acrylics, thin glazes are a good way of conveying the delicacy of petals and leaves; the colours mix optically on the support, creating subtle blends that would be difficult, to achieve in the palette. The equivalent technique in gouache is to work thinly in semi-transparent washes, allowing each wash to modify the wash beneath.

Working wet into wet in any medium will enable you to convey subtle shifts of tone. In gouache and thin acrylics, you can allow the colours to flow and merge on the support of their own accord; although the technique is somewhat unpredictable, with practice you will have more control. In thicker acrylics and in oils, working wet into wet allows the artist to blend the

paint on the support, feathering brush-strokes to create subtle transitions in tone.

Textures are important too. Exploit the full range of textural techniques at your disposal – drybrush work for linear details on petals or leaves, scumbling one colour over another, dabbing paint on thickly with a painting knife to convey a mass of small flowers.

If you're painting several flowers together, choose a viewpoint that allows you to see some of them from the side, rather than straight on. This makes it easier to see the structure of the bloom and make it look three-dimensional; it also makes for a more interesting painting.

Alchemilla and roses ▼
This lovely oil study effectively contrasts both colour and shape, the delicate and "frothy" stems of bright, yellow green alchemilla providing a lovely foil to the more rounded forms of the roses.

Autumn day ▲
Here, the foliage makes a natural-
looking frame for the church, the
warm-coloured leaves enhancing the
pale colour of the stonework.

Lovage, clematis and shadows ▶
In this scene, it the shadows cast by the
stems, rather than the flowers that
caught the artist's eye. They bring the
painting to life.

> **Tip**: Match the technique to the
> flower: use delicate wash or glazing
> techniques for delicate flowers and more
> robust textural techniques for more
> substantial blooms.
> • Subtle coloration, where one colour
> blends imperceptibly into another, is best
> painted using wet-into-wet techniques.
> • Flowers and leaves have a strong
> underlying structure, which should always
> be shown. These structural differences are
> what separates one species from another.

Irises

You don't have to venture outside to create convincing nature studies: in this project, a vase of irises is painted to look like flowers growing in the wild. They have been given a background of subtle washes and brushstrokes of yellowy green that give the impression of a luxuriant flower meadow. The artist has also selected a low viewpoint, so that we feel as if we are lying down in the grass and looking through the stems. You could try the same approach with other relatively tall wild flowers, such as poppies.

This project also gives you the chance to explore an interesting means of creating subtle paint textures by pressing plastic food wrap into wet paint: who would have thought that something so mundane could be put to such creative use? The paint seeps into the crinkles in the food wrap; when it is completely dry the food wrap is removed, leaving behind linear marks that perfectly convey the delicate veining and papery texture of the flower petals.

You need to work quickly, while the paint is still wet, so tear off appropriately sized pieces of food wrap in advance. Stretch them out between your fingers and place them on the wet paint following the direction in which you want the lines to run. Tap them down gently with your fingertips – but do not rub, or you will smudge the paint. Above all, wait until you are sure that the paint is completely dry before you attempt to remove the food wrap. The technique is a little unpredictable, but that is part of its charm and the results more than repay the effort.

Materials
- *140lb (300gsm) rough watercolour paper*
- *Pencils: 2B or water-soluble*
- *Acrylic paints: ultramarine blue, light blue violet, dioxazine violet, Hooker's green, medium yellow, Hooker's green deep, yellow ochre, titanium white*
- *Brushes: medium round; fine-tipped round or rigger*
- *Plastic food wrap*
- *Masking fluid*
- *Ruling drawing pen*

The set-up
Place your flowers in a vase and experiment until you find an arrangement you are happy with. You will probably need to remove or add stems to get the effect you want, but remember to look at the spaces between the stems, as well as at the flowers, as the placement of the stems is an important part of the composition. You may also need to adjust the height of the vase in order to get the right viewpoint: the flower heads should be slightly above your eye level.

Nowadays, you can buy good-quality very convincing-looking artificial flowers. Although they do not have the same texture and subtlety of colour as real flowers, they can show you the botanical structure very clearly. If you are interested in painting flowers, it is also worth building up your own personal collection of gardening books and cuttings from magazines and seed catalogues to use as reference material for your paintings.

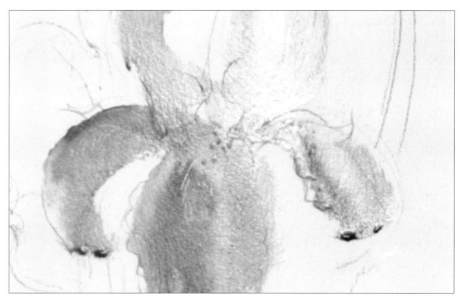

1 Lightly sketch the flowers in pencil. Here, the artist used a blue water-soluble pencil to delineate the flowers; the linear marks will disappear when paint is applied. However, an ordinary graphite pencil would work just as well.

2 Using a ruling drawing pen, stipple masking fluid into the flower centres and mask the edges of the leaves where they catch the light. Allow the masking fluid to dry completely. Working on one flower at a time, brush clean water over the petals. Drop a watery mixture of ultramarine blue and light blue violet into the damp area, adding a touch of dioxazine violet on the lower petals. The paint will spread within the damp area, and the colours will merge with no harsh edges.

3 Working quickly while the paint is still wet, stretch a small piece of plastic food wrap out in your fingers and press it gently but firmly on to the first petal. Make sure that you lay the food wrap out following the direction of the striations in the petals.

4 Repeat the process until all the petals have been covered. Provided the wash is still wet, you can lift off the food wrap two or even three times to reposition it if necessary, but remember that you will lift off paint every time you do this: take care not to get paint on to areas outside the petals.

▶

5 Begin painting the leaves in Hooker's green, adding medium yellow for the lighter-coloured leaves. While the paint is still wet, brush a little dioxazine violet along the shaded lower edge of some leaves; this helps to show how the leaves twist and turn, and it provides a visual link with the colour of the flowers. Paint the papery sheaths at the base of the petals in a mixture of yellow ochre and Hooker's green and cover with plastic food wrap, taking care not to dislodge any of the food wrap from the petals as you do so.

6 When you are sure that the petals are completely dry, carefully peel off the food wrap. Note how some of the paint has been blotted off, creating the delicate papery texture and veining that is so characteristic of iris petals.

Tip: Colour is one of the ways in which you can imply distance in your paintings, as colours look paler the further away things are from the viewer. In this project, the use of different tones of green for the iris stalks and leaves makes it seem as if we are looking through a sea of waving stems and grasses, with only the flowers and leaves in the immediate foreground being in sharp focus and strong colour – a simple but effective technique.

7 Mix a pale, watery yellow-green from medium yellow, yellow ochre, Hooker's green and a little light blue violet. Wet the background with clean water. Don't worry if some water goes over the painted areas; the paint will not lift off provided it is completely dry. With flowing, calligraphic strokes that imitate the shape of the leaves, brush the yellow-green mixture over the right-hand side of the background. Paint a few more strokes in Hooker's green deep, which is darker, to imply that these leaves are closer to the viewer.

8 Add light blue violet to the previous yellow mixture and, as in the previous step, paint loose, leaf-like strokes to the left and right of the central flowers in order to create an atmospheric, but realistic-looking background. While the paint is still wet, apply plastic food wrap over these areas in exactly the same way as you did for the petals, stretching it taut from top to bottom so that it runs in the same direction as the leaves.

9 When the paint is completely dry, remove the plastic food wrap. In the space between the two main flowers, brush in the shape of another flower head, using a paler, bluer mixture of the previous flower colours. Because it is paler than the main flowers, it gives the impression of being further away. Leave to dry.

10 Using the same green mixtures as before, brush in more dark leaves in both the foreground and the background. Look carefully at the points where leaves overlap: it should be obvious which leaves are in front and which are behind.

11 Using the tip of the brush, paint fine lines of dioxazine violet on to the petals of the top right-hand flowers to reinforce the striations in the petals that were left when you pulled off the plastic food wrap. Your brushstrokes should be delicate squiggles rather than flat applications of colour, as this helps to create texture. Leave to dry, then rub off the masking fluid from the centres of the flowers.

Assessment time

Now it is time to assess exactly how much more work you need to do in order to complete the painting. At present, the flowers merge into the background because the colours are a little too pale: the tones need to be strengthened and darkened in order to make the flowers stand out more. In the final stages of a painting, it is often necessary to adjust the tones that you put down to begin with. The flowers are also somewhat soft and indistinct – the delicate textures created by pressing the food wrap into the wet paint need to be reinforced with some careful and subtle brushwork. It would be very easy to overdo things and lose the subtlety of the painting, so mix and assess any darker tones very carefully before you apply them to the support and use a fine-tipped brush so that you can control where you place your brushstrokes.

The flowers are too soft and indistinct.

12 Brush medium yellow into the flower centres. Strengthen the petal colour using the same ultramarine blue and light blue violet mixtures as before. Note that the upper petals are bluer in tone than the lower ones.

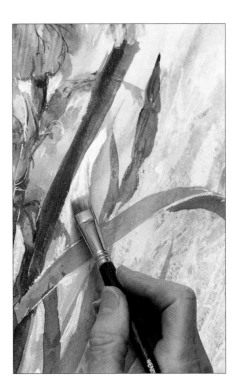

13 Mix a pale, opaque yellow from medium yellow and titanium white. Brush this into the spaces between the leaves where necessary to reinforce the shapes of the leaves.

The finished painting
This is a delicate study that captures the characteristics of the flower to perfection. The clever use of tone, with darker tones in the foreground and lighter ones further back, has created a convincing sense of depth. The papery texture of the petals is created through a combination of calligraphic brushstrokes and blotting off paint.

Soft yellows and greens provide a natural-looking background that allows us to concentrate on the flowers.

The vertical lines on the translucent petals are created by pressing plastic food wrap into wet paint and lifting it off when dry.

Calligraphic brushstrokes, made using only the tip of the brush, define the petal edges.

The leaves twist and turn over one another, enlivening the composition.

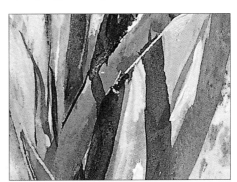

Floating leaf

A landscape doesn't have to be a grand, panoramic view that stretches far away to the distant horizon: little details, such as this brightly coloured leaf floating in a mountain stream, can be just as appealing and atmospheric.

Although this little stream and rocks might not, at first glance, appear to contain much colour, there are many subtle variations in tone, and it is essential that you take time to observe the scene closely and work out where these changes in tone occur.

This looks like a very simple scene, but in practice you would have to be very lucky to find a leaf floating exactly where you want it to be! However, one of the advantages of painting is that you can alter reality to make a better picture – so feel free to introduce a leaf where none exists in real life or to change the angle at which it lies across the stream to make a more interesting composition.

One of the advantages of using gouache for a scene such as this is that, because you can paint light colours over dark ones, you can put in the highlights on the sparkling water right at the end, when everything else is in place. If you were using pure, transparent watercolour, you would have to reserve the white of the paper for the highlights or scratch off paint using the tip of a craft (utility) knife, with the risk of damaging the surface of the support. With gouache, you can spatter on white paint for a random effect or dot it on with a fine paintbrush for a more controlled look. Use permanent white gouache for highlights: it has better covering power than zinc white, which is best reserved for mixing with other colours in order to lighten them.

Materials
- *Watercolour board*
- *HB pencil*
- *Masking film (frisket paper)*
- *Craft (utility) knife*
- *Gouache paints: cadmium yellow deep, sap green, ultramarine blue, flame red, indigo, Vandyke brown, permanent white*
- *Brushes: medium round, fine round, old toothbrush*

The leaf ▶
Here, the artist decided to make a floating leaf the main centre of interest. It makes a bold splash of colour against the darkness of the water.

The stream ▼
When you are painting a moving subject, such as this flowing stream, a photograph can help you to capture the way the light plays on the scene.

Tonal sketch ▼
Making a tonal sketch helps you to work out the main areas of light and shade before you begin painting, although it does not have to be as detailed as the one shown here.

2 Continue dotting ultramarine blue over the water, brushing the colour over the rocks and leaving the highlight areas untouched. Leave to dry.

1 Lightly sketch the scene on watercolour board. Stick masking film (frisket paper) over the image and, using a craft (utility) knife, cut around the floating leaf. Peel the masking film off the rest of the image, leaving the leaf covered. Using a medium round brush and a dilute mix of cadmium yellow deep, paint the underwater rocks. Mix a dilute bluish green from sap green and ultramarine blue and dab it over the water area.

Tip: If you are worried about cutting into the board when you cut out the leaf for the mask, trace the entire underdrawing on to tracing paper and stick masking film over the trace. Put the trace on a cutting mat, cut out the mask, and position the masking film on the relevant part of the image.

3 Using the tip of the craft knife to lift up the edge of the masking film, peel the film off the leaf.

4 Mask off everything except the leaf. Brush very dilute cadmium yellow deep over the leaf. Add more pigment to the mixture and drop it into the centre of the leaf, allowing it to spread of its own accord. Brush flame red, wet into wet, around the edges.

5 Brush flame red over the tips of the leaf, leaving the central portion of the leaf light yellow. Dip an old toothbrush into the flame red paint, hold it over the leaf, and gently pull back the bristles to spatter droplets of paint on to the leaf.

Tip: Practise on a scrap piece of board first until you are confident that you can make spatters the right size. Do not pull too hard: the spatters should be small.

▶

6 Gently peel off the masking film to reveal the whole painting.

7 Mix a dark blue from indigo and Vandyke brown and, using a fine round brush, paint around the leaf and surrounding rocks. Brush small strokes of cadmium yellow deep over the rocks to deepen the tone.

Assessment time
The colours and shapes of the leaf and rocks have been established, as have the areas of water. This is a good start, but the image still looks rather flat and two-dimensional at this stage. There is little sense of depth, and it is a little hard to tell which rocks are above the water level and which ones are covered by the flowing stream. The painting is also rather static: there is also no real feeling of movement in the water.

More sense of movement is needed in the water. This can be achieved with fine brush strokes.

These rocks lack form. Greater definition of the rock and the water next to it will help.

8 Using a fine round brush, go over the water again with ultramarine blue paint, sharpening the outline of the leaf. With short brush strokes, brush a mixture of cadmium yellow deep and flame red over those areas of the rocks on the left that stick up above the water.

9 Using indigo, paint shadows on the rocks.

10 Brush small, curved strokes of permanent white into the water around the leaf to indicate ripples.

11 Mix together sap green and ultramarine blue and build up the texture in the strip of greenish water at the base of the image. Continue building up the tones and textures over the whole image. It is better to work across the whole painting than to concentrate on just one area, otherwise you risk overworking one part at the expense of the rest.

The finished painting

This is a simple little scene that many landscape artists might pass by in favour of a grander view. It is a study in contrasts – the softness of the water versus the solidity of the rocks, the vibrant colour of the leaf versus the muted tones of the water. The brushwork is controlled, with the brush strokes in the water following the direction of the water flow to create lifelike ripples. Note how the main centre of interest – the leaf – is positioned slightly off centre and at an angle to add interest to the composition.

Water flows over the rocks in this area, and so the detail and texture are deliberately subdued.

Wet-into-wet spatters and wet-on-dry applications combine to create a lively texture on the leaf.

This rock stands clear of the water; more detail and texture are evident here than in the submerged rocks.

Tulips in glass vase

In this simple still life, a bunch of pink and green parrot tulips has been placed in a turquoise glass vase that complements their shape beautifully. When you paint a subject like this, with overlapping shapes and twisting stems, remember to look at the spaces between as well as at the flowers and stems themselves. Note, too, how the water in the vase distorts the shapes of the stems and how the semi-opaque glass affects the colours of anything seen through it.

In order for the form of the flowers to stand out, opt for a neutral, plain-coloured background. Here, the vase was placed on a window ledge in front of a sheer muslin curtain, which diffuses and softens the light it lets through, creating a subtle contre-jour effect. But even though the background is a plain colour, you will see that there are lots of tonal contrasts within it. Even the gentlest of folds in the

fabric will create shadows that you must render tonally. Try half-closing your eyes when you look at the scene, as this will subdue the detail and make it much easier for you to assess where the tonal changes occur.

One difficulty with painting cut flowers is that they either wilt and perish or turn upwards towards the light. You may find that your still life is not still at all: over a period of just a few hours, the flowers may droop and change position. If you're painting in oils, and creating a painting over a number of painting sessions several days apart, this can be a real problem. Work quickly in the early stages to make sure you capture the position, shape and colours while the flowers are at their best – or take photos for reference.

Another problem with this set-up is that natural light can change considerably over several sessions. As you can see from the

photographs below, in the first session the light was very overcast and uniform. During the final painting session a few days later, strong sunlight cast oblique shadows on the scene, and the artist incorporated them into the final painting to add drama and interest. This project, above all else, is an exercise in painting the effects of light.

Materials

- *Stretched and primed canvas*
- *Oil paints: olive green, raw sienna, viridian, yellow ochre, Indian yellow, lemon yellow, titanium white, madder lake, Caesar purple, cadmium red, cobalt blue, cerulean blue, phthalocyanine turquoise*
- *Turpentine*
- *Brushes: selection of small and medium filberts and sables*
- *Rag or absorbent kitchen paper*

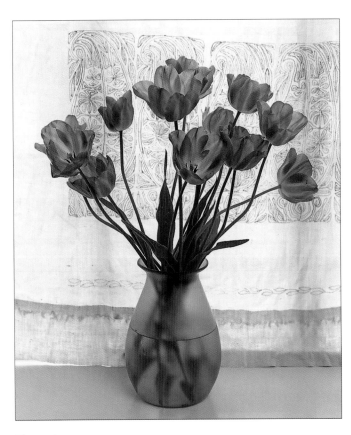

The set-up
A vase of spring tulips, loosely arranged, was placed on a window ledge. The light coming from outside, which was soft and uniform, was diffused still further by the semi-transparent muslin curtain. As a result, there are few shadows in the scene and the colours are muted.

Change in lighting
At the beginning of the final painting session, the sunlight outside was much stronger than it had been originally. The glazing bars of the window cast interesting oblique shadows on the muslin curtain, which the artist decided to exploit in the final painting.

1 Mix a dull brown from olive green and raw sienna. Using a small brush, draw the overall lines and shapes of the flowers and vase. Put in the glazing bars, which can be seen through the curtain, and the window ledge.

> **Tip**: Put down guidelines, such as a vertical line through the centre of the vase. Turn your painting upside down to check the shapes. This makes it easier to see objects as geometric forms.

2 Mix greens for the leaves and stalks (viridian, yellow ochre and Indian yellow for the warmer dark and mid-toned areas, and viridian, lemon yellow, and titanium white for the more acidic areas). Mix pinks for the flowers (madder lake and white, with a touch of blue for the cooler shades, and Caesar purple and white). Vary the proportions of the colours to give a good range of tones. Using a mid-toned and a slightly bluer green, put in the stalks and leaves protruding from the vase. Start to block in the flowers.

3 Continue to block in the flowers, adjusting the proportions of the colours in your mixes to get the right tone. Because of their position in relation to the light, some flowers are much warmer in tone than others: add a little cadmium red for these mixes. In others, where petals overlap, a deeper shade of purple can be seen. Work methodically and spend as much, if not more, time looking at your subject as you do looking at the canvas: you need to assess tones and colours continually as you work.

4 Using various dark greens, paint the stalks. Mix a bright blue from cobalt blue and titanium white and put in the darkest areas at the top of the vase, and the water line halfway up. Mix cerulean blue and white for the light blues in the top half of the vase, and a greener blue for the water.

5 Paint the stems that are underwater, using a darker green. The shapes are slightly distorted by being seen through water; the colours are also softened by the opaque glass of the vase. You can create these effects by blending the green into the underlying wet paint.

▶

6 Mix a pale, creamy brown colour by adding Indian yellow and white to the bright green that you used you used on the flower heads. Begin blocking in the dark panel in the centre of the muslin curtain behind the flowers, taking care not to obliterate the lines of the glazing bars completely.

7 Outside the central panel, the curtain is lighter in tone. Mix blue and white and scumble the colour on loosely, allowing some of the toned ground to show through to create the texture of the woven fabric. Paint more of the stems, noting how they twist and turn over one another.

8 At this point, the artist decided to alter some of the flowers on the left, as he felt that the painting was weighted too heavily towards the right-hand side. Because oil paint stays wet for so long, you can simply wipe it off with a rag soaked in turpentine and re-paint if necessary.

Assessment time

The basic elements and tones of the composition have been established, but more form is required. Both the vase and the flowers look rather flat at this stage and tend to merge into the background.

The flowers look flat and two-dimensional.

There is no sense of depth to the window ledge.

9 Using the tip of a small sable brush, sharpen the edges of the flowers to give them a crisp outline, and put in some linear detail on the petals, using a deep purplish pink and a bright, acidic green as appropriate. You can see that the flowers almost immediately begin to take on more of a sense of form and to stand out more clearly from the neutral-coloured background; they are no longer merely flat blocks of colour.

10 Continue to refine the details, working on the tonal changes within the petals to create some sense of depth and form. As before, half-close your eyes as you look at the scene, to see where the changes in tone occur.

11 Paint the deep hem of the curtain in the same mixture that you used for the central panel. The darker colour means that the flowers have something to register against. Don't obscure the glazing bars; they will be reinforced later.

12 The vase is reflected in the window ledge. Put in this reflection, using slightly curved brushstrokes that echo the form of the vase, and leaving some gaps to create the effect of shimmering light. Work more pale blue into the vase interior, carefully painting around the flower stems.

13 Using the same neutral background colours as before, work around the vase, sharpening the edges and softening any areas that are overly blue. Using a pale, neutral blue-grey, strengthen the glazing bars that can be seen through the fabric.

▶

14 Strengthen the greens of the stems in the water. Look at the negative spaces between the stems as well as at the stems themselves. Reinforce the shadow cast by the vase on the window ledge.

15 At this point, the artist realized that the shape of the glass vase was not quite right. He also felt that the blue he had used for the vase was not vibrant enough. Because the paint was still wet, he was able to scrape it off with a knife and repaint, using a mixture of phthalocyanine turquoise and white. He then wiped off some of the turquoise paint with a piece of absorbent paper to soften the colour and create the effect of light being diffused through the glass.

16 Gently stroke a paler version of the phthalocyanine turquoise and titanium white mixture used in Step 15 over the top half of the vase, blending the colours wet into wet, to heighten the effect of soft, diffused light coming through the glass.

17 In the final stages, the lighting changed. Mix a range of greys from cobalt blue, white and a little Caesar purple and put in the shadows cast by the glazing bars. Warm up the neutral background mixture by adding Indian yellow, and scumble it over the background.

The finished painting

This is a charming study in the effect of diffused and reflected light. The texture of the translucent petals and the opacity of the blue vase have been beautifully captured in soft blends of colour. Loose scumbles of various warm- and cool-toned neutral mixes convey both the texture of the muslin curtain and the effect of light shining through it.

The glazing bars can still be seen through the curtain, although their shadows are more prominent.

The glass distorts the shapes and softens the colour of any objects that can be seen through it.

Linear details applied using the tip of a fine brush help to bring the flowers forwards in the scene.

Woodland path

This project is about interpreting what you see and conveying the mood of the scene, rather than making a photorealistic rendition. That does not mean that observation is not important, however. When you are painting a scene like this, look at the overall growth patterns. Are the tree trunks tall and straight or do they lean at an angle? Do the branches droop and spread on either side of the trunk, like weeping willows, or is the foliage weighted towards one side, like maples and Scots pines? Is the shape of the tree basically conical (like many conifers) or rounded (like oaks)?

Look at where the shadows fall, too – and remember that the shape made by the shadows should match the shape of the objects that cast the shadows. Above all, make sure that the shadows are dense enough, as the contrast between the dark and the brightly lit areas is what gives the work a three-dimensional quality.

This scene also gives you the useful opportunity to explore many different textures – the tangled undergrowth and criss-crossing branches, the rough texture of the path and the peeling bark on the trees. Again, try to capture the mood rather than placing every detail precisely. Spatters of paint convey the rough texture of the ground, while the colour of the tree trunks and the patterning of the bark call for more carefully placed brush strokes.

Here the artist also added a few small pieces of collage in the final stages. This is optional, and you may think that the image does not need it; however, provided you do not overdo things it is well worth experimenting with simple techniques like this, as they can bring an added dimension to your work.

Materials
- *Watercolour paper primed with acrylic gesso*
- *4B pencil*
- *Masking fluid*
- *Medium-nibbed steel dip pen*
- *Gouache paints: phthalocyanine green, brilliant yellow, raw umber, raw sienna, zinc white, scarlet lake, jet black, phthalocyanine blue*
- *Brushes: large wash, small round, old toothbrush*
- *Newspaper*
- *Gum arabic*

The scene
Although there is no real focus of interest in this scene, the textures and the contrasting shapes (the sweeping curve of the path against the strong vertical lines of the tree trunks) make it very rewarding to paint. The shadows over the foreground also add interest.

1 Using a 4B pencil, sketch the scene, putting in as much detail as you feel you need. Your underdrawing will help you to keep track of where things are once you start applying the paint.

Tip: You do not need to get all the branches in exactly the right place in your underdrawing, but you should try to be faithful to the general patterns of growth and the rhythms of the scene. Although this is a fairly loose, impressionistic painting, it must look convincing – but it is also important to try to capture a sense of spring-like growth and energy in the scene.

2 Using a medium-nibbed steel dip pen and masking fluid mask the lightest trunks and branches. Also mask any branches that are lighter than their immediate surroundings, even if they are brown in colour rather than a light, silvery grey. Using an old toothbrush, spatter some masking fluid over the undergrowth. Leave to dry: this won't take long, but it is essential that the masking fluid is completely dry before you apply the first washes of colour.

3 Before you begin the painting stages, take some time to make absolutely sure that you have masked all of the light-coloured areas of branches and foliage that need to be protected. Even though gouache is opaque and it is perfectly possible to paint light colours over dark ones, such corrective measures should only be used as a last resort – otherwise you run the risk of losing some of the freshness and spontaneity of the painting.

4 Mix a dilute, bright green from phthalocyanine green and brilliant yellow. Using a large wash brush, put in broad horizontal strokes for the band of undergrowth that runs across the centre of the scene. Mix a duller green from phthalocyanine green and raw umber and repeat the process in the foreground. For the tree trunks in the background, put in vertical strokes of raw sienna and raw umber, occasionally adding some green to them.

5 Mix a dilute yellowish brown from zinc white and raw umber and brush the mixture lightly over the earth in the foreground, allowing some of the support to show through to create some texture in this area. The earth on the far right, behind the band of undergrowth, is warmer in tone, so paint this in raw sienna. While the paint is still wet, touch a little scarlet lake into it so that it spreads of its own accord.

6 Mix a very dark greenish black from jet black, phthalocyanine blue and phthalocyanine green and paint the little stream in the background. Add raw umber to the mixture and paint the cast shadows on the ground.

7 Add more phthalocyanine green to the mixture and paint the shapes of the trunks in the background. Using the bright green mixture from Step 4, spatter colour over the foreground for the low-growing plants alongside the path.

8 Roughly cut masks from newspaper the same shape as the largest cast shadows on the ground and lay them in position. (There is no need to stick them down.) Mix brilliant yellow with white, load an old toothbrush with the mixture, and spatter it over the foreground, pulling the bristles back with your fingertips.

9 Repeat the spattering process with a mixture of white and raw umber to create the rough, pebbly texture of the path in the foreground. When the paint is dry, remove the newspaper masks: the scene is now beginning to take on more depth and texture.

10 There are some warm, pinkish tones on the path, so mix scarlet lake and white and lightly spatter a little of the mixture over the foreground. Leave to dry completely, then rub off all the masking fluid.

Tip: When you have removed a little of the masking fluid, squash it together into a ball and rub it over the surface of the painting like an eraser. Any remaining fluid will stick to it – and it is a lot easier on your fingertips.

Assessment time
Now that you have removed the masking fluid, it is easier to see what must be done to complete the painting. Although the general shapes are all there, at this stage the painting lacks depth: you need to increase the density of the shadows.

The exposed areas are too stark and bright and contain no detail.

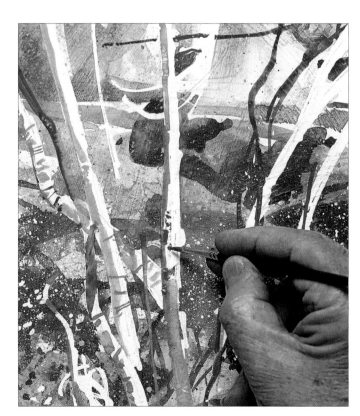

11 Mix a pale brown from raw sienna and white. Using a small round brush, paint the shaded sides of the exposed tree trunks. Add raw umber to the mixture and paint the shadows cast on the tree trunks by other branches.

12 Mix brilliant yellow with a little phthalocyanine green and, using a small round brush, dot in the yellow flowers in the undergrowth, making the distant dots slightly smaller than those in the foreground.

13 Using various versions of the dull green mixture from Step 4, paint the exposed grasses on the bottom right of the painting, keeping your brushstrokes loose and flowing.

Tip: Vary the greens, as this will look more natural. Some grasses are more mature than others, and some are more shaded, hence the variations in tone.

14 The yellow flowers in the centre look a little too vibrant, so tone them down by dotting some of the dull green mixture from the previous step into this area. Put in some solid areas of green, too, obliterating the exposed whites and re-establishing any shadow areas that have been lost on the grasses. Using mid-toned browns, reinforce the lines of trunks in the background.

15 You might consider the painting finished at this point, but here the artist decided to enhance the three-dimensional quality of the upper part of the image by incorporating a little collage. If you do this, take care not to overdo it, or the result could end up looking messy and overworked.

16 Paint strokes of branch-coloured paint on a piece of scrap paper and leave to dry. Cut out curving, branch-shaped pieces and brush a little gum arabic on to the reverse side. Position the pieces on the painting and brush gum arabic over the top to fix them in place. Leave to dry. (The advantage of using gum arabic is that, unlike ordinary glue, it can be painted over if necessary.) The collage element adds depth and texture to the image.

The finished painting

This is a lively and atmospheric painting of a woodland path in dappled sunlight. The strong vertical lines of the tree trunks and the diagonal lines of their shadows give the picture a feeling of energy that is echoed by the textural details and bold applications of colour. The palette of colours chosen by the artist is muted but natural looking. Although the scene looks deceptively simple, there is much to hold the viewer's attention.

Spatters and dots of colour convey the texture of the path and the tiny flowers.

The use of collage on some of the branches is subtle but effective.

Carefully placed brushstrokes are used for the grasses and tree bark.

Painting animals and birds

One of the most obvious difficulties of painting animals and birds is that, unlike people, they cannot generally be persuaded to sit still. However, with relaxed subjects such as a sleeping cat or dog or a rabbit held in its owner's arms, you stand at least some chance of being able to put down the basic lines of the 'pose' before the animal moves. Sketching a family pet that you already know well is a good introduction to animal painting.

When you feel ready to paint moving animals and birds, spend time simply watching them, without even attempting to put brush to canvas. You'll soon see patterns emerging – the way a cat licks itself clean, or a dog sniffs at the ground, or a caged bird hops from one perch to another, for example. Try to fix these movements in your mind so that you can incorporate them into your paintings. Reference photos may help, provided you don't rely on them too much – but there is no substitute for sketching from life, even though your first attempts will probably not be very successful.

A little knowledge of basic anatomy is a great help, just as it is when you're painting people. Knowing the names of all the joints and muscles won't get you very far, but having some idea of how the joints are articulated or the sequence in which an animal's legs move will. Until the early days of photography, for example, jumping horses tended to be depicted with their front legs stretched out in front and the back legs stretched out behind; think of the paintings of George Stubbs (1724–1806). Now we know that they launch themselves off their back legs with their front legs brought close to the body and tucked in tightly.

When it comes to painting feathers and fur, aim to convey a general impression rather than capture every single hair, otherwise your painting will look fussy and overworked. Painting wet into wet is a good way to achieve this as you can work a second fur colour into or over a first to create subtle blends on the support. Drybrush is also a good technique for rendering fur and feathers, especially when used with a fan blender.

Swans ▼
The ripples in the water and the sparkling sunlight give this painting a lovely sense of movement. Note how many different tones have been used to paint the birds' white feathers.

Tip: The more time you spend observing animals, the better your paintings will be. Make quick sketches whenever you can.
• Animal and bird movements are often repetitive. Analyse this so that you can anticipate what the animal is likely to do, as this will make it easier to draw them.
• As with human portraits, the eyes are very important: get their position and shape right and you're well on the way to a successful portrait.

Studio window reflected ▲
Anyone who owns a cat will recognize this as a typical cat "pose" – legs sprawled out, head erect and ears pricked for the slightest sound. Quick sketches of such poses made while the animal is at rest are a good way of capturing its character and personality.

Turning fish ▶
The artist has skilfully conveyed the movement of the fish with his treatment of the light shining on the water and the ripples on the surface.

Sleeping cat

It is lovely to be able to put your painting skills to good use to paint a portrait of a cherished family pet. Because you know your animal so well, you will easily be able to find a pose that sums up its character and personality, and a painting like this would make a wonderful gift for another family member. Here, the artist combined a quick snapshot of the sleeping animal with a background of brightly coloured leaves from his garden.

There are several ways to approach painting fur. In a water-based medium such as acrylic, you might choose to apply loose, impressionistic washes of colour wet into wet, so that the the paint blends on the support to create subtle transitions from one tone to another, perhaps lifting off colour with clean water to create lighter-toned areas. In this project, we build up the colour in thin glazes, gradually darkening the shaded areas until the right density is achieved, with each layer of paint being allowed to dry before the next one is applied. Use short brushstrokes that follow the direction in which the fur grows, and an almost dry and very fine brush. This creates the impression of individual strands of hair and is a particularly effective way of conveying the texture of the fur.

The project also gives you the chance to practise masking. Because you need to mask out large areas in the early stages of the painting, use masking film (frisket paper) rather than tape or fluid. Masking film is used by draughtsmen and is available from most good art supply stores. To ensure that the film adheres firmly to the support and that no paint can seep under the edges, choose a smooth surface, such as illustration board.

Materials
- *Illustration board*
- *Masking film (frisket paper)*
- *Craft (utility) knife*
- *Gouache paints: cadmium yellow deep, flame red, burnt sienna, Vandyke brown, indigo, permanent white*
- *Brushes: medium round, fine round*

The cat
The artist used this photograph as reference material for the cat's "pose" and the colour and texture of its fur. However, the striped wallpaper does not make a very attractive background.

The background
These leaves provided a colourful and natural-looking background against which to position the cat.

Compositional sketch

When you are combining two or more references in a painting, you must give some thought to the relative scale of the different elements. Make a quick sketch, in colour or in black and white, before you begin painting.

Tonal sketch

This cat is predominantly ginger in colour, but there are many different tones within the fur. Making a tonal sketch in pencil or charcoal enables you to work out not only the different tones but also the composition of your painting.

1 Referring to your initial sketch, lightly draw the cat using an HB pencil, indicating the main clumps of fur. Draw the veins on the leaves. Place masking film (frisket paper) over the sketch and, using a craft (utility) knife, cut around the outline of the cat. Peel away the masking film that covers the leaves.

Tip: The last thing you want is for paint to seep under the masking film on to the area of the painting that you are trying to protect. Working in one direction only, wipe a clean tissue or soft rag over the film to smooth out any wrinkles and ensure that the film is stuck down firmly. It is best to work towards the cut edges of the film.

2 Using a medium round brush, brush cadmium yellow deep gouache paint over all the leaves to establish the underlying colour. While the paint is still wet, rinse your brush in clean water and drop flame red over the tips of the leaves. The two colours will combine wet into wet to make a warm orange, creating soft-edged transitions of colour. It is important that you leave the paint to dry completely before you move on to the next stage; like watercolour, gouache paint dries very quickly, so this should only take a minute or two, but if you want to speed up the drying time, you can use a hairdryer on a warm setting. Hold the dryer well away from your painting so that you do not accidentally blow the red paint away from the tips and into the centre of the leaves.

▶

4 When you are sure that the paint is completely dry, carefully peel the masking film back from the cat. You can see how the leaves have crisp edges: it is easy to achieve this using a mask.

3 As you can see, the yellow and red merge together on the support in a way that looks completely natural. It does not matter if the colour is darker in some parts of the leaves than in others.

5 Mix a warm, yellowish brown from cadmium yellow deep and burnt sienna. Using the medium round brush, brush this mixture over the cat, leaving the white fur untouched. Your brushstrokes should follow the direction in which the fur grows. Leave to dry.

Tip: If you are worried about accidentally splashing colour on to the leaves when you paint the cat, cover them with the masking film that you removed in Step 1.

6 Mix a rich, chestnut brown from burnt sienna and Vandyke brown. Using a fine round brush, put in the dark fur on the cat's face, again using short brushstrokes that follow the direction in which the fur grows. Mix a darker brown from Vandyke brown and indigo and paint the dark fur around the edges of the ears.

7 Use the same colour to paint the dark spaces between the leaves, so that the individual leaves stand out clearly.

8 Using Vandyke brown and the tip of the brush, start putting in the dark brown markings on the cat's face.

Assessment time

Brush a dilute version of the cadmium yellow deep and burnt sienna mixture used in Step 5 over the non-white areas of the cat's face to warm up the tones overall.

The painting is starting to take shape but more detail is needed to bring out the roundness of the face and the texture of the fur.

The fur contains little texture.

The cat merges with the background; the leaves do not yet look like leaves.

▶

10 Mix flame red with a little cadmium yellow deep. Using a medium round brush, brush this colour over the leaves, allowing some of the original pale yellow colour to show through as the veins in the leaves.

9 Mix a very pale pink from flame red and permanent white and brush it on to the tips of the ears, which are slightly pink, and the tip of the nose. Using the Vandyke brown and indigo mixture from Step 6, put in the dark spaces between the claws. Add more water to the mixture. Brush clean water over the foreground and dot the indigo and Vandyke brown mixture into it.

11 Using the same mixture, build up the intensity of the red, taking care not to go over the veins.

Tip: Remember that gouache looks slightly darker when it is dry than it does when it is wet, so wait until the paint is dry and assess its colour before you add another layer. It is better to build up the density of colour gradually: if you make the leaves too dark, they will overpower the cat, which is the main focus of the painting.

12 Using the indigo and Vandyke brown mixture, deepen the colour of the leaves. Note that the edges of the leaves are slightly serrated; use a fine brush to paint the serrations. Use the same colour to darken the very dark fur markings and the outlines of the mouth and nose.

The finished painting

This is a slightly whimsical but very appealing painting of a cherished family pet in a characteristic "pose". The leafy background provides a colourful foil for the animal and focuses attention on its face, while delicate brushwork captures the texture of the fur.

Here, the artist has used white gouache and a very fine brush to put in the whiskers and more fur texture in the final stages. It is up to you how much detail you put in: you might choose to build up the tones and textures more than has been done here.

The texture of the fur has been built up gradually, using fine brushstrokes that follow the direction in which the fur grows.

Small details – the pink of the nose and the outline of the mouth – convey the character of the sleeping cat.

The richly coloured, textured autumn leaves provide a simple but dramatic backdrop to the portrait.

Farmyard chickens

Whether you are painting wild or domesticated animals, it is interesting to paint them in their environment – in this case, a corner of a farmyard, where the chickens are allowed to range freely, pecking at grain.

Before you begin painting, spend time observing how the chickens move. Although you might at first imagine their movements to be completely random, you will soon see a regular pattern emerging – a staccato rhythm of strutting and pecking, stabbing at the ground to pick up grains of wheat before throwing the head back to swallow. Try to fix this rhythm in your mind, as it will help you to anticipate what the bird is likely to do next. Look, too, at the way the movement of the head and legs affects the rest of the bird's body: when the head is tilted down, the rest of the body tilts up – and vice versa. Regardless of whether you are painting from life or from a photograph, accurately capturing the angle of the body in relation to the head will give added veracity to your work.

This project also gives you the opportunity to practise a number of different ways of capturing texture in acrylics. By applying very thin layers of paint in glazes, you can build up the slightly uneven coloration of the rusting cartwheel in the background, while the woodgrain on the wheelbarrow is painted using just the tip of the brush. Spatters of paint on the gravelled area in the foreground and thick dabs of paint applied to the chickens with a painting knife also add textural variety to the painting.

Materials
- *300gsm (140lb) NOT watercolour paper*
- *HB pencil*
- *Masking fluid*
- *Ruling drawing pen*
- *Acrylic paints: yellow ochre, raw sienna, burnt sienna, cadmium orange, cadmium yellow, Hooker's green, burnt umber, light blue violet, violet, cadmium red*
- *Brushes: medium chisel or round*
- *Small painting knife*

The scene
Although this is an attractive scene, with lots of detail, the colours are a little subdued. The artist decided to boost the colours a little and make more of the sense of light and shade in her painting, in order to make a more interesting and better balanced picture.

1 Using an HB pencil, make a light underdrawing of the scene to use as a guide. Dip a ruling drawing pen in masking fluid and outline the chickens. Mask out the lightest areas – the white dots on the chickens' feathers, the bright wisps of straw on the ground, and the brightest bits of foliage. Leave the masking fluid to dry completely.

2 Mix up a dilute wash of yellow ochre and another one of raw sienna. Using a medium round brush, wash yellow ochre over the side of the wheelbarrow and the background foliage. Loosely brush raw sienna over the foreground, which is darker than the rest of the image. These two loose washes of warm colour establish the overall colour temperature of the scene.

3 Brush raw sienna over the fence posts. Add burnt sienna to the mixture and paint the triangular-shaped wedges inside the background cartwheel. Use the same mixture for the shaded portion of the wheelbarrow wheel and for the wooden supporting struts and handle of the barrow. In effect, what you are doing in these early stages is making a tonal underpainting of the scene.

4 Brush a dilute mixture of cadmium orange over the straw lying in the wheelbarrow and on the ground, using short brushstrokes. Brush the same colour over the spokes of the cartwheel and the body of the brown hen perched on the wheelbarrow handle. Add more pigment to the mixture and paint the brown hen's head.

Tip: Always vary the length and direction of your brushstrokes to suit the subject. Here, broad sweeps are used to block in large areas such as the wheelbarrow, while short, individual strokes are used for the wisps of straw.

5 Mix a yellowy green from cadmium yellow and a little Hooker's green and wash this mixture over the bushes behind the fence. Add a little burnt umber to the mixture in places to get some variety of tone. Leave to dry.

▶

7 Mix a purplish grey from light blue violet and burnt sienna and paint the shaded wheelbarrow interior and the shaded parts of the fence posts.

Tip: Neutral greys can be created by mixing together two complementary colours. This scene is relatively warm in temperature, and therefore two warm colours (light blue violet, which is a warm, red-biased colour, and burnt sienna, a warm reddish brown) were combined to produce the shadow colour. For a cool shadow colour (a snow scene, for example), mix cool, blue-biased complementaries.

6 Mix a dark green from Hooker's green and burnt sienna and dab this mixture over the bushes, twisting and turning the brush to create leaf-shaped marks and allowing some of the underlying yellowy green from the previous step to show through. Note that some of the foliage pokes through the gaps and obscures part of the wooden fence posts.

8 Mix a warm grey from violet and a little Hooker's green and paint the grey chicken on the wheelbarrow, leaving the beak untouched. Add burnt sienna to the mixture and paint the dark shadow areas inside the cartwheel and on the struts of the wheelbarrow.

9 Paint the dark feathers of the white chicken in light blue violet and brush the same colour loosely over the grey chicken on the wheelbarrow to create some variety of tone in its feathers. Mix a warm brown from burnt sienna and cadmium orange and paint the rim of the cartwheel. Brush burnt sienna over the body of the brown chicken on the wheelbarrow, allowing some of the underlying colour to show through. Splay out the bristles of the brush and brush thin lines of burnt sienna over the foreground.

10 Paint the chicken combs in cadmium red. Mix a very dark green from violet and Hooker's green and dot this colour into the foliage, wherever there are really dark leaves or shaded areas. The different tones of green help to create a feeling of dappled light in the foliage.

11 Mix a purple shadow colour from violet and light blue violet, adding lots of water so that the mixture is very dilute, and brush this colour over the shadowed area underneath the wheelbarrow. When this is dry, brush thin, straw-like strokes of yellow ochre over the foreground.

Assessment time

Rub off the masking fluid. At this stage, the painting still looks rather flat and lifeless; the wheelbarrow and chickens do not stand out sufficiently from the background. You need to add more texture to both the foliage and the foreground areas and increase the contrast between the light and dark areas.

Stronger tonal contrast is needed in the foliage to help create a sense of light and shade.

More texture is needed – particularly on foreground elements such as the wheelbarrow.

12 Mix a very dilute yellowy green from cadmium yellow, Hooker's green and a little yellow ochre and brush the mixture over the greenery at the top of the image to warm it a little. Brush pale yellow ochre over the exposed straw in the wheelbarrow and in the foreground. Brush very pale light blue violet over the grey chicken to tint the exposed dots.

13 Brush the purple shadow colour from Step 11 over the foreground to deepen the shadows and improve the contrast between the light and dark areas.

15 Spatter dark brown mixture over the foreground. Use the same colour to paint dark feathers on the brown chicken. Mix cadmium yellow with yellow ochre and apply light, textured strokes to the foreground.

14 Mix a dark brown from burnt sienna and violet and, using the tip of the brush, "draw" in the wood grain on the wheelbarrow. Use the same colour to paint the "ruff" of dark feathers on the white chicken in the foreground.

16 Dot thick white paint over the grey chicken's body and yellow ochre over the brown chicken's body.

The finished painting

This is a charming farmyard scene that exploits the versatility of acrylics to the full. The paint on the rusty metal cartwheel and wooden wheelbarrow is applied in a similar way to watercolour – in thin layers, so that the colour and subtle variations in tone are built up gradually. Elsewhere – on the bodies of the chickens and the straw-strewn ground, for example – relatively thick impasto applications create interesting textures that bring the scene to life.

Note how the application of layers of colour, wet on dry, creates the texture of rusty metal.

Thick paint, applied using the tip of a painting knife, shows the texture of the ruffled feathers.

A range of techniques, from fine spatters to thick impasto work, is used to paint the pebble-strewn ground and loose straw.

Tropical butterfly

Both butterflies and moths belong to the scientific order Lepidoptera, which means "scale-wing" in Latin, and most butterfly wings are covered with tiny, individually coloured scales arranged in partially over-lapping rows, like tiles on a roof. Butterfly houses give you the chance to see all kinds of exotic, brilliantly coloured and patterned species that you might never be able to encounter in the wild. This peacock pansy butterfly (*Nymphalidae precis almana*) is indigenous to Nepal and neighbouring regions and is characterized by the eye-spots on the wings, which act as a deter-rent to potential predators.

The artist selected a smooth-surfaced board for this study in oils, for two good reasons: first, he wanted this to be a reasonably detailed painting and a smooth surface allows you to put in small details without the paint spreading and sinking into the support; second, he did not want the texture of the support to show through in the final painting.

To speed up the drying time and enable you to complete the painting in one ses-sion, use a medium to which a drying agent has been added, such as drying linseed oil.

As each scale on the wing is different-ly coloured, you will find infinitely subtle gradations of tone. One way of convey-ing both the texture of the wings and the subtlety of the colour shifts is to stipple the paint on, using the tip of the brush, to create optical colour mixes in the same way that the Pointillist painters such as Georges Seurat (1859–91) did. However, although some inks and liquid water-colours can come close, it is difficult to match the intensity of iridescent colours with even the brightest of pigments.

Materials
- *Smooth-surfaced board*
- *HB pencil*
- *Oil paints: chrome yellow, cadmium orange, geranium lake, brilliant pink, titanium white, ultramarine blue, turquoise blue deep*
- *Turpentine (white spirit)*
- *Drying linseed oil*
- *Brushes: selection of fine rounds, filbert*

The butterfly
With its dramatic eyespots and brilliant colouring, this peacock pansy butterfly makes an appealing subject for a painting. However, the artist decided not to include all the flowers, as he felt they detracted from the butterfly. It is perfectly permissible to leave out certain elements of a scene in order to make your painting more dramatic.

1 Lightly sketch the butterfly in HB pencil. It is entirely up to you how much detail you put into your underdrawing, but including the veins and the fringe-like pattern around the outer edge of the wings will make it easier for you to keep track of where you are in the painting.

2 Using a fine round brush and alternating between chrome yellow and cadmium orange, start putting in the basic colour of the wings. Thin the paint with turpentine (white spirit) and mix it with drying linseed oil so that it is the consistency of single (light) cream.

Tip: Use a different brush for each colour, so that you do not have to keep stopping to clean brushes.

3 Continue until all the yellow is complete, looking closely at your subject to see the different tones. You may need to turn the support around and use a mahl stick to keep your hand clear of wet paint. If you do not have a mahl stick, you can improvise one by taping rags around one end of a thin piece of wood or dowelling, as the artist did here.

4 Mix a range of bright pinks from geranium lake, brilliant pink and titanium white and start painting the flowers on which the butterfly is resting. Mix a dark, purplish blue from ultramarine blue and geranium lake and start putting in the background, taking care not to get any colour on the butterfly. Again, use a mahl stick, if necessary, to keep your hand clear of any wet paint.

5 Continue painting the background, carefully cutting in around the flower tendrils.

Tip: When you are clear of the butterfly and flowers, switch to a larger brush to enable yourself to cover the background more quickly.

6 Using the same colours that you used for the flowers and background, start putting in some of the dark detail on the butterfly, using short brush strokes to convey the texture of the scales on the wings.

7 Paint the "eyes", using cadmium orange and the purple/pink mixture from the previous step and stipple the colour on with the tip of the brush to create an optical colour mix. Note that there are bluish-purple patches next to the two largest eyes: add more white and ultramarine blue to the mixture for these areas. Paint the "fringe" around the outer edge of the wings in oranges and pinks, as appropriate.

▶

Assessment time

The main elements of the painting are in place. All that remains is to add more fine detailing to the butterfly and complete the surrounding flowers and background, working carefully and methodically. Although the artist had originally intended to include the flowers to the right of the butterfly, at this point he decided that they would detract too much from the painting of the insect.

The dark background acts as a foil to the butterfly. Keeping its edges irregular adds to the informality of the study.

The detail is beginning to take shape; features like this are best put in during the final stages, when the underlying colours and shapes have been established.

8 Using a fine brush and the same pinks and purples as before, paint the flowers on the left-hand side, gradually working down the painting. Paint as much of one colour as you can while you have it on your brush. When you have finished the flowers, paint the dark background.

9 Paint the body of the butterfly, blending the colours on the support so that the brushstrokes are not visible.

10 Continue painting the dots of colour on each side of the body. Although the dots are clustered more densely near the body, the same colours also run along some of the veins. Finish painting the "eyes" on the left-hand side of the butterfly, using the same colours as before.

11 Mix a bright blue from turquoise deep blue and white and dot it into the whites of the "eyes". The patterning is now beginning to stand out strongly. Reinforce the orange areas around the two largest eyes with cadmium orange, deepening the colour with geranium lake where necessary.

The finished painting

Although this was never intended as a photorealistic painting, pointillist-style dots of colour help to capture the iridescent quality of the wings – something that cannot be achieved easily in paint. Much of the painting consists of a single layer of paint, which is appropriate for the thin, delicate structure of the insect. Note the clever use of different lengths of brush stroke to create texture: longer, blended strokes are used for the furry body, while short strokes and tiny stipples convey the individual scales on the wings. The artist has also used some artistic licence in reducing the number of flowers so that the butterfly is more clearly defined against the dramatic, dark background.

The flowers are loosely painted but echo some of the colours in the butterfly.

Different lengths of brush stroke create different textures.

The butterfly stands out clearly against the dark background.

Painting landscapes

Landscapes are probably the most popular of all subjects to paint. Each season has its own mood and colours, each scene its own unique features.

The most important thing to decide on when painting a landscape is what constitutes your focal point. A grand panoramic view is all very well, but there must be something that holds the viewer's interest. Do not include too much, however, or your painting will look jumbled. Feel free to simplify and leave out any elements that do not contribute to the overall effect.

Once you have selected your focal point, decide where to place it within the picture area. Placing a subject in the centre of the picture is generally best avoided, as it tends to result in a static image – although there may be times when you deliberately do this to create a calm mood. One placement that almost always works well is "on the thirds" – roughly one-third of the way into the painting from both the horizontal and the vertical edge.

Use lines or curves, either real or implied, to help lead the viewer's eye to the focal point. You might, for example, choose a viewpoint that allows a river to snake its way through the scene in an S-shape, or have a secondary point of interest on an implied diagonal line.

Another important consideration is how much sky to include. Beginners often place the horizon line right across the middle of the image, which cuts the picture in half and looks rather boring. If you have an interesting sky, emphasize it by placing the horizon low down; conversely, a sliver of sky (or even no sky at all) places the emphasis on the land.

To convey a sense of scale and distance in landscapes, keep in mind that objects that are further away look smaller than those that are close by. Colour is another way of implying distance, as colours tend to look paler the further away they are. Texture, too, plays a part: more textural detail should be evident in the foreground than in the background.

Crooked tree against the dazzle ▼
The strong diagonal line that runs upwards through the painting from the bottom left gives a sense of energy to this very simple seaside scene.

The view from here ▲
The lines of the fence and furrows in the snow curve inwards, leading our eye to the focal point of the image, which is placed on the third.

River Laune, Ring of Kerry ▶
The main interest is in the rolling hills and sinuous curve of the river. Note how the sky is reduced to a relatively small sliver near the top of the frame.

> **Tip**: Use a full range of techniques to suggest different surface textures.
> • When working in impasto, incorporate plenty of direction strokes to help the eyes read the shape of the thing being painted.
> • Use a degree of artistic licence to improve a scene by leaving things out or even by adding elements that are not there in reality.

Stormy sky

Although the small strip of land and the high-rise buildings at the base of this picture provide an essential calm, static point on which the viewer's eye can rest, the main interest undoubtedly lies in the dramatic and bleak, stormy sky, with its dark, billowing clouds and the warm glow of the setting sun shining through them.

When you are painting clouds, remember that you need to make them look like solid, three-dimensional objects, not mere wisps drifting across the sky. You should also follow the rules of perspective and make clouds that are far away smaller than those that are directly overhead.

For this project use acrylic paint thinly, flooding the paper with generous washes of dilute colour. The aim is to create an impressionistic scene, with no hard edges to the clouds and very little detail in the buildings. Let the paint do as much of the work for you as possible, such as puddling at the base of damp areas to form darker tones at the base of the clouds. Soften paint edges by dabbing off any excess with a paper towel.

Materials
- *Watercolour board*
- *Acrylic paints: cerulean blue, alizarin crimson, burnt sienna, ultramarine blue, lemon yellow, titanium white*
- *Brushes: large round, medium flat*
- *Household plant sprayer*
- *Flow improver*
- *Absorbent paper towel*

The scene
The warm glow of an evening sunset contrasts dramatically with the glowering purple of the storm clouds in this scene. Note the complementary colours – purple and yellow – which almost always work well together. Although the silhouetted buildings along the skyline occupy only a small part of the picture area, they are critical in giving a sense of scale to the image.

1 Using a household plant sprayer, spray clean water on to the board over the areas that you want to remain predominantly blue. (You could brush on water – but the spray gives a more random, less controlled coverage.)

2 Mix a few drops of flow improver into cerulean blue paint. Using a large round brush, drop the paint into the areas that you dampened in Step 1; it will spread and blur to give a soft spread of colour.

3 Scrunch up a piece of clean paper towel in your hand and dab it on to the blue paint to soften the edges.

4 Mix a warm purplish blue from cerulean blue and alizarin crimson. and brush it over the land area at the base of the image with the large round brush. Mix a neutral purplish grey from burnt sienna and ultramarine blue. Spray clean water over the left-hand side of the painting and quickly drop in the neutral colour, allowing the paint to pool at the base of the damp area, as storm clouds are darker at their base.

5 Soften the edges of the clouds by dabbing them with a paper towel, as in Step 3. While the paint is still damp, dot in more of the dark mixture in the top right of the painting.

6 Using a watery version of the neutral purplish grey mixture from Step 4, brush in a dark line above the purplish base, adding more burnt sienna nearer the horizon to warm up the tones. Allow the paint to dry. Mix a warm purple from burnt sienna and ultramarine blue and, using a medium flat brush, make broad, rectangular-shaped strokes for the high-rise buildings along the horizon line, varying the tones so that the nearer buildings are slightly darker than those that are further away. Use strokes of different thicknesses to create a natural-looking variation in the shapes and sizes of the buildings.

Assessment time
You have now established the basic framework of the image and the main areas of colour – the blue of the open patches of sky, the dark storm clouds that dominate the scene, and the thin sliver of land with its high-rise buildings at the base. However, for the painting to look convincing, the clouds should be made more three-dimensional.

The clouds are soft-edged but do not appear to have volume.

Varying the tones of the buildings helps to create a sense of recession.

7 Mix a pale but warm, yellowy orange from lemon yellow, titanium white and a little burnt sienna. Brush this mixture into the breaks between the clouds, making horizontal brushstrokes that echo the direction in which the clouds are being blown in order to create a sense of movement in the sky. This adds warmth to the horizon and makes the dark storm clouds stand out all the more dramatically.

8 Continue adding this warm yellowy orange, adding more burnt sienna to the mixture as you get nearer the horizon; the sun is sinking, so the colours are warmer nearer the horizon. Mix an opaque blue from cerulean blue and titanium white, and brush this mixture over the top of the sky, smudging the paint with your thumb to soften the edges and get rid of any obvious brushstrokes.

9 Dip a small piece of paper towel into the warm purple mixture that you used in Step 6 and squeeze out any excess moisture. Lightly stroke the paper towel over the yellow area just above the horizon to create streaks of storm cloud.

Tip: You could apply the paint with a rag or a sponge instead of a piece of paper towel. All these tools create a more random, spontaneous-looking effect than a brush and are very appropriate for a natural scene such as this.

10 Dab light opaque blue into the very dark area at the top of the picture, using your fingertips. Mix a purple from cerulean blue and burnt sienna and swirl it around the light area in the centre of the paper to darken it and give the clouds more of a feeling of depth. Mix a pale, warm yellow from burnt sienna, lemon yellow and titanium white and stroke on shafts of light coming down from the clouds with your fingertips. Using a flat brush, block in the shapes of the nearest buildings on the skyline; using warmer, darker tones in this area will make these buildings look closer to the viewer.

The finished painting

This is a convincing representation of a stormy sky at dusk. The colours are allowed to spread on damp paper and pool naturally, creating soft-edged shapes that are darker at their base and thus appear to have volume. Although the colour palette is limited and based mainly around the complementary colours of purple and yellow, the clever use of different tones of purple in the buildings at the base of the image creates a sense of recession.

The silhouettes of the buildings along the skyline are painted as simple rectangles of colour, exploiting the natural shape of the flat brush.

Purple and yellow are complementary colours and almost always work well together. Here, they create a warm-toned yet dramatic-looking composition.

There are no harsh-edged colours in the sky – dabbing the wet paint with a paper towel helps to remove any potentially distracting brushmarks.

Rocky landscape

This is a dramatic and impressive vista of rocky outcrops surrounded by open moorland, which falls away rapidly to the sunlit landscape below.

The scene covers a wide area and there are lots of things to hold your attention – but don't allow yourself to get too caught up in the detail. Think instead about the general characteristics – hard rocks next to soft, springy vegetation, deeply shaded areas such as the side of the rock that is facing us versus brightly lit sections such as the fields.

There are also lots of different colours, from the muted grey of the rocks and the purple heather to the bright blue of the sky. You may find that it helps to half-close your eyes when you look at the scene, as this will help you to see it in terms of blocks of colour rather than as a landscape that consists of many different individual elements.

There are several things to bear in mind when trying to convey a sense of scale and distance. First, the further away things are, the smaller they look. Note the crag in the middle distance, for example: it's actually about the same height as the foreground crag, but because it's quite a long way away, we perceive it as being smaller.

Colour plays a part in this, too: generally, things that are further away appear paler in tone, so remember to make your colours paler as you move towards the horizon.

Finally, foreground elements should contain more detail and texture than those in the background.

Gouache is an interesting choice of medium for a scene like this. The slightly chalky nature of the paint makes the shaded rocks look almost hazy, as if our vision is affected by the bright sunlight that is streaming in from the right. At the same time, the opacity and covering power of gouache enable you to paint very precise, crisp highlights without any of the underlying colour showing through.

Finally, toning the ground a bright yellow, as the artist has done here, means that you begin your painting from a warm mid-tone, which sets the overall colour temperature of the sunlit scene and contributes to the mood of the painting.

Materials
- *Illustration board*
- *B pencil*
- *Gouache paints: cadmium yellow deep, cadmium orange, cadmium red, phthalocyanine blue, spectrum violet, cerulean blue, permanent white, Naples yellow*
- *Brushes: large wash, small round, large round bristle*
- *Rag or absorbent kitchen paper*

The scene
There are many interesting textures to paint in a scene such as this, from the springy heather that covers much of the ground, to the hard gritstone rocks. The lighting is important, too: note how the contrast between light and shaded areas helps to convey the direction of the light and makes what might otherwise seem like flat areas of vegetation appear three-dimensional.

1 Using a B pencil, make a light underdrawing of the main elements of the scene, indicating the outline of the rocky outcrops. Make a series of flowing pencil strokes across the foreground to indicate shading within the moorland vegetation.

2 Mix a generous wash of cadmium yellow deep gouache paint and another one of cadmium orange. Using a large wash brush, loosely wash cadmium yellow deep over the whole of the paper. While the first wash is still slightly damp, brush cadmium orange over the bottom right of the painting – the rocky outcrop in the foreground. Leave to dry. The colour is uneven but it provides a lovely warm, toned ground on which you can develop your painting.

3 Mix a dark purple from cadmium red, phthalocyanine blue and spectrum violet. Using a small round brush loaded with very little paint, brush the mixture over the pencil marks made in Step 1. Holding the brush almost vertically, make short, spiky strokes for clumps of grass in the foreground and longer, calligraphic strokes on the rocky outcrop in the background. Block in the rocky outcrop in the foreground.

> **Tip**: The use of a dark, solid colour (as an underpainted colour) on the large rocky outcrop in the foreground makes it appear closer to the viewer.

4 Mix a mid-toned greyish blue from cerulean blue, permanent white and cadmium orange. Using a small round brush again, brush in the horizon line and broken horizontal strokes to the left of the second outcrop of rock. You are starting to establish the undulating bands of vegetation that run across the scene. The use of a cool colour here helps to convey a sense of distance.

5 Now mix a dark green from phthalocyanine blue, cadmium yellow deep and a little of the purple mixture from Step 3. Using a small round brush, dab this mixture on loosely to create a triangular wedge of green for the wooded area in the middle distance, allowing the underlying colour to show through. Dab the same colour across the foreground hill.

> **Tip**: Whenever you are painting vegetation, make your brushstrokes follow the natural direction of growth: use short, vertical brushstrokes for the trees in this scene.

▶

6 Continue dabbing on green and the purple mixture from Step 3, as in the previous step, in order to build up texture in the vegetation.

Tip: Don't attempt to place each stroke precisely. Your aim should be to build up a general impression of loose, scrub-like plants rather than a botanically accurate rendition.

7 Using the purple mixture again, but varying the proportions of the colours in the mixture, block in the rocky outcrops, using vertical brushstrokes of varying lengths and widths and allowing some of the underlying rock colour to show through for the lighter-coloured rocks.

8 Continue darkening the colour of the foreground vegetation, using the same mixtures as before. Add permanent white to the purple mixture to lighten it and make it more opaque, and brush small horizontal strokes over the low-lying area beyond the second outcrop. This establishes the colour of the main vegetation in this area – the flowering heather. The area is so far away that the general colour is sufficient: there is no need to put in lots of textural detail.

9 Add more permanent white and a little phthalocyanine blue to the opaque purple mixture from step 8 and dab it over the shaded areas of the foreground rocky outcrop, allowing some of the underlying colour to show through. This helps to create the texture of the rocks, which have cracks and crevices running through them.

10 Mix a bright green from cadmium yellow deep and phthalocyanine blue. Brush small horizontal strokes of the mixture over the low-lying, sunlit fields in the background.

Assessment time
The contrast between the shaded and sunlit parts of the image is now becoming more apparent and the scene is taking on a convincing sense of depth and perspective. Note, in particular, how toning the ground yellow has imparted a warm glow to the sunlit areas.

This bright green nestles between the two rocky outcrops and draws our eye to them.

The yellow in this area looks unnatural but gives a warm glow to this sunlit area.

The rocks are beginning to take form, but will require more texture if they are to look convincing.

11 Mix a brownish pink from cadmium red, permanent white, Naples yellow and spectrum violet and dot and dab it over the foreground vegetation. As before, your aim is to create a general impression of the small, scrubby plants.

12 Using a small round brush, apply short strokes of permanent white and a little cadmium yellow deep to highlight areas of the rocks. This emphasizes the structure of the rocks, which have very distinct facets.

Tip: Permanent white gouache has good covering power, which makes it ideal for painting opaque highlights.

13 Continue to build up texture in the vegetation. Using a small, almost dry round brush loaded with permanent white paint, make a series of light vertical brushstrokes over the foreground to imply gently the taller grasses among the heather. Foreground texture is one of a number of ways in which the artist can imply that such areas are physically closer to the viewer.

14 Using a large round bristle brush, scumble dilute permanent white over the sky. Although gouache is opaque, the fact you are using a dilute mixture means that the white is slightly modified by the underlying yellow, which will give the impression of warm afternoon sunlight in the sky.

15 Mix a bright blue from cerulean blue and permanent white and brush it loosely over the sky, leaving some white shapes for clouds. Skies are never uniform in colour because of the effects of light, so darken the mixture by adding a tiny amount of cadmium red and put in a few strokes of this colour here and there to create some tonal variation. While the paint is still wet, gently dab a clean cloth or a piece of absorbent kitchen paper over the sky to soften the brushstrokes and blend the colours together on the support, so that the transition from one tone to the next is virtually imperceptible.

16 Reinforce the clouds with permanent white where necessary to make them stand out a little more dramatically, remembering to make them smaller as they recede towards the horizon.

The finished painting

Repeat the previous two steps if necessary to build up more colour in the sky. This is a strong and dramatic landscape that exploits the characteristics of gouache to the full. Wet-into-wet applications of paint in the sky create soft-edged cloud formations, giving a sense of movement that is counter-balanced by the solidity of the rocky landscape below. Texture in the vegetation is achieved through drybrush work and short brushstrokes. The natural opacity and chalky nature of gouache paint can be seen in the way the artist has painted the rocks, which look convincingly three-dimensional.

Note how darker tones are used for the undersides of the clouds, which are in shade. Clouds, just like any other feature of the landscape, are three-dimensional and it is important to give them volume.

Texture is a feature of this painting. The artist has used drybrush work and small dabs and dots of paint to create a convincing impression of the scrubby moorland vegetation.

Bright highlights are achieved with short strokes of opaque permanent white, while the shaded sides of the rocks are painted in an appropriately dull, chalky mixture of purplish grey.

Sunlit beach

This simple-looking scene of an almost deserted beach on a bright summer's day gives you the chance to paint two of nature's most fascinating subjects – moving water and sparkling sunlight.

Painting the sea is an interesting challenge: how can you capture the constant ebb and flow of the water? As always, the more time you spend observing the scene the better. Although the movement of the waves may seem random, if you stand still and watch for a while you will soon see a pattern. Look at the shapes that the waves make as they roll in towards the shore and try to fix them in your mind.

One of the risks of painting in bright sunshine is that your eyes can be dazzled by the intensity of the light, with the result that you tend to make the scene too high-key. Instead of capturing the brightness of the scene, as you expected, you will find that your painting simply looks bleached out. Look for tonal contrasts within the scene and balance bright areas with dark, cooler shadows. The dark passages will have the effect of making the light areas look even brighter.

When painting highlights, don't try to put in every single one or your work will look overly fussy. Half-close your eyes: this reduces the glare, enabling you to break down the pattern of light more easily and put in just the key highlight areas.

Finally there is the question of how to paint the sky. If you're painting *en plein air* and the clouds appear to be fleeting, you may want to put them down quickly to capture the effects, whereas with a relatively static scene, you might concentrate on the land first. But remember that clouds have volume: look for the lights and darks within them to make them look three-dimensional.

Materials
- *Stretched and primed canvas*
- *Oil paints: olive green, cobalt blue, titanium white, alizarin crimson, cerulean blue, burnt umber, Indian yellow, cadmium red, black, lemon yellow*
- *Turpentine*
- *Brushes: small filbert brush, selection of small hogshair and sables*

The scene
The tide has receded, leaving shallow inlets illuminated by bright sunlight and large areas of exposed sand – an interesting contrast of colours and textures.

1 Using a thin mix of olive green, 'draw' the cliffs on the horizon, the lines of the waves and the little channels. At the outset the artist decided to add a small dog to the scene to focus the viewer's attention. Add its outline and shadow now.

2 Mix a bright, light blue from cobalt blue and titanium white. Using a small filbert brush, loosely scumble the mixture over the shallow areas of water in the foreground of the scene. Add a little alizarin crimson to the mixture to make it slightly more purple in tone, and brush in the line of cliffs along the horizon in the background. Mix a paler blue from cerulean blue and titanium white and use this mixture for the most distant area of sea.

3 Add a tiny amount of burnt umber to the purplish blue mixture from Step 2 and blend this colour, wet into wet, into the darkest parts of the sea – the undersides of the waves that roll in towards the shore. Mix a rich, dark sand colour from burnt umber and Indian yellow and scumble this mixture over the sand, blending in a few strokes of cadmium red here and there, and adding purple for the very darkest lines along the edges of the water channels.

4 Add a little burnt umber to the bright blue mixture from Step 2, and scumble it over the deepest areas of the foreground water. Using short, vertical brushstrokes, loosely scumble various sand colours over the shallowest parts of the water, where the underlying sand is clearly visible.

5 Continue putting in the sand areas in the middle distance. Note that some areas are pinker and warmer than others; adjust the mixtures on your palette as appropriate. Block in the dog and its reflection in a dark mixture of olive green, black and a little burnt umber.

▶

6 Continue to build up the tones in the water, using the same purplish blues as before to emphasize the darker areas. Overlay pale blue paint over the water-covered sand in the foreground, blending the vertical brushstrokes that you put down in the earlier stages to create the impression of sand seen hazily through shallow water.

7 Now start to work on the sky. Put in the clouds first, using light- and mid-toned greys mixed from burnt umber, cobalt blue and titanium white in varying proportions. Warm or cool the mixtures as necessary by adding a touch of pink or blue. Put in the bright blue of the sky using a mixture of cobalt blue and titanium white.

8 Use a darker version of the olive green, black and burnt umber mixture that you used in Step 5 to reinforce the shape of the dog and its reflection in the wet sand.

9 Now start to put in some of the reflected highlights on the crests of the waves, dotting in little specks of white tinged with yellow to give the impression of sunlight glancing off the surface of the water.

Assessment time

Now that the main elements and colours are in place, take time to assess the tonal balance of the painting as a whole. Although the orange of the sand and the blue of the sea are complementary colours and give the scene a lot of energy, they are both predominantly mid-tones. You need to reinforce the sense of sunlight within the scene – and, paradoxically, the way to do this is to make the dark areas darker, so that they form an effective contrast to the brightly lit parts.

You need to create a sense of sunlight sparkling on the water.

The sand is little more than a block of colour at this stage; it needs more texture.

10 Darken the water channels in the foreground, using the same purples and blues as before.

Tip: Don't add any solvent to the paint for this process: using the paint straight from the tube means that it is relatively dry, so the colours do not turn muddy even though you are overlaying paint on a layer that it still wet.

11 Touch some very pale yellow (made by mixing lemon yellow, a little Indian yellow and titanium white) into the top of the clouds to create the effect of warm sunlight.

12 Look at the colours within the sea: it is by no means a uniform blue. Add a little purple to your blue mixes to put in the darkest parts of the small waves as they break on the shore. Loosely block in the figures, using a purplish blue-black. As they are silhouetted, with the sun behind them, little detail is discernible. Add a hint of yellow to titanium white and put in fine lines to create highlights on the foam-tipped wave crests.

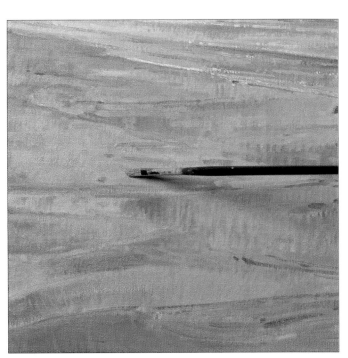

13 Continue putting lights and darks into the sea area, using small strokes and dotting in the highlights. In the deeper channels in the foreground water, use loose vertical strokes of a mid-toned blue to create the sense of light shimmering in the water. The brushstrokes will soon be blended out, but their direction is important as it helps to give the effect of sunlight glancing off the water.

14 Continue working on the foreground area, using the sand colour and blue mixes tinged with purple as appropriate. Gently and gradually blend the wet paint on the canvas and smooth out the brushstrokes.

15 Create more variety and texture in the exposed sand area by dotting in other colours – a light yellow mixed from lemon yellow and white, and burnt umber lines and dots. Dot the pale yellow mixture that you used in Step 12 over the foreground to create the effect of sunlight sparkling on the water.

16 Mix a bright blue from cobalt blue and titanium white and scumble it over the top of the sky to darken it and allow the clouds to stand out more dramatically. The use of a dark colour at the top of the picture holds the viewer's eye within the frame, while the loose brushstrokes help to give an impression of movement in the sky.

The finished painting

This is an attractive painting of an almost deserted beach in summer. Lively brushstrokes convey the dark clouds scudding across the sky, and loose scumbles of colour over the water also help to convey a sense of movement. The viewpoint has been carefully chosen so that the wedge-shaped areas of sand in the foreground balance the composition and lead our eye through the painting. Although the dog and the silhouetted figures in the middle distance occupy only a small part of the scene, their position (roughly on the thirds) means that our eye is drawn to them.

The use of complementary colours (blue and orange) imparts a sense of energy.

Specks of yellow create the effect of warm sunlight glancing off the water.

The dog occupies only a small area, but its position means that our eye is drawn to it.

Rolling hills

Sometimes when you are painting a landscape, a single element – a lone tree, a waterfall, a farm building, for example – attracts your attention; at other times, it's the sheer scale and drama of a broad panorama that draws you. In the latter case, however, it can be hard to evoke the same feeling of awe in the viewer that you felt on beholding the scene – and more often than not, the reason for this is that you have failed to provide a focal point in your image.

In the landscape shown here, gently rolling hills sweep far away into the distance in an idyllic rural setting that gives no hint of the hustle and bustle of the modern world. But even in the most rural of settings, evidence of former industries can often be seen. Although the quarries in which they were cut have long since ceased to operate, these abandoned millstones provide the artist with a focal point for his painting. Without them, the scene would look like an empty stage set, with nothing to hold the viewer's interest.

This project uses acrylic paint in a similar way to traditional watercolour, with the colours being built up gradually in thin glazes, so that each layer is modified by the underlying colours. It also incorporates a wide range of textural techniques, from drybrush work to less conventional methods such as pressing bubble wrap into the paint and dabbing on paint with your fingertips. There is no "right" or "wrong" way to apply paint to the support: use whatever tools you have to hand to create the effect you want.

Materials
- Card primed with acrylic primer
- B pencil
- Acrylic paints: cadmium yellow, cadmium red, phthalocyanine blue, burnt umber, magenta, titanium white, cobalt blue, cerulean blue
- Brushes: medium round, small round
- Rag
- Bubble wrap

1 Using a B pencil, make a light underdrawing of the scene, taking care to get the ellipses and angles of the millstones right.

The scene
The millstones are the focal point of the painting. Note how they form a rough triangle, positioned just off centre at the base of the image, leading the viewer's eye up the line of the hill and back down again to the foreground. When you paint a scene like this, make sure you spend time selecting the best viewpoint.

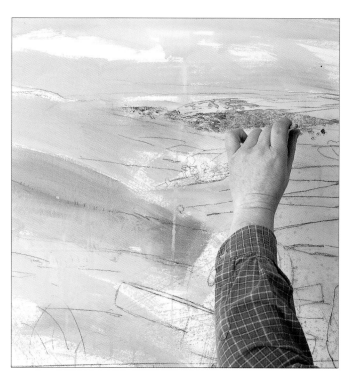

2 Using a rag, spread cadmium yellow acrylic paint straight from the tube over the support, leaving a few gaps in the sky area for clouds. Drop a little cadmium red over the centre left of the image and blend it into the yellow paint with the rag so that the two colours merge on the support, creating an orange, wedge-like shape. Leave to dry.

3 Mix a dark green from cadmium yellow and phthalo-cyanine blue. Using a medium round brush, scumble the mixture over the wooded hillside in the middle distance to give a generalized impression of trees. While the first green is still damp, add a little more blue to the mixture and dot this in for the darkest areas of green.

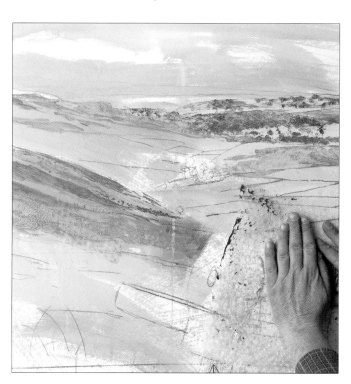

4 Mix a dull but warm orange from cadmium yellow, cadmium red and a little burnt umber and brush it over the distant escarpment on the left of the image and over the fields in front of the wood. The warm colour helps to bring this area forwards in the image.

5 Using a medium round brush, apply a thin glaze of magenta in a broad stroke over the slope of the hill on the left. Add a little phthalocyanine blue to the mixture and paint the crest of the escarpment behind it. While the paint is still wet, gently press bubble wrap into it to create some texture.

▶

6 Add a little burnt umber to the dark orange mixture from Step 4 and brush it loosely over the bottom left corner of the painting. While the paint is still wet, lift off some of the colour by "drawing" the shapes of grass stems with the tip of a paintbrush.

7 Darken the hillside, using the same colours as in Step 5. Press bubble wrap into burnt umber paint and then press the bubble wrap across the bands of orange and magenta on the left to create loose, textured dots that echo the growth pattern of the vegetation. Paint the fence posts using a dark, reddish brown mixed from phthalocyanine blue and burnt umber. Mix a dark purple from cadmium red and phthalocyanine blue and brush it over the shaded sides of the mill-stones. For the darkest stones, use phthalocyanine blue.

8 Dot in the shapes of the isolated trees in the middle distance, using the same dark orange that you used to paint the fields. Following your initial pencil marks, mark out the field boundaries in burnt umber. Roughly block in the buildings in the middle distance in magenta. Brush a broad sweep of magenta over the hill to the right of the buildings and wipe a rag over it to blur the colour.

9 Brush titanium white over the sky area, allowing a hint of the underlying yellow to show through to maintain the overall warm colour temperature of the scene. Re-establish the highlight areas on the ground by smearing on titanium white paint with your fingertips, which gives a more spontaneous-looking and random effect than applying the paint with a brush.

Assessment time

It is becoming clear which parts of the scene are in shadow and which are brightly lit, and the underlying yellows and oranges give a warm glow to the whole scene. Now you need to concentrate on putting in the greens and browns of the landscape and on building up the textures.

Note how the colours become paler in tone the further away they are.

The yellow used as a base colour on these sunlit fields will modify any glazes that are applied on top.

More texture is needed in the grasses in the immediate foreground.

10 Reduce the starkness of the white areas by brushing over them with a thin glaze of the appropriate colour – cobalt blue over the wooded area, burnt umber over the shaded parts of the hillsides, and various yellow-orange mixtures over the sunlit fields. Note how the scene becomes more unified as a result.

11 Mix a bright green from cadmium yellow and cerulean blue and, using a medium round brush, paint over the mostly brightly lit fields in the middle distance. Note that some of the fields contain crops, so leave the underlying orangey brown colour in these areas and take care not to go over the field boundaries.

12 Add a little more titanium white to the mixture to lighten it and paint the most distant fields. Mix a neutral brown from cadmium yellow, cadmium red and phthalocyanine blue and use it to tone down the reddish areas on the hill to the left, which look too harsh.

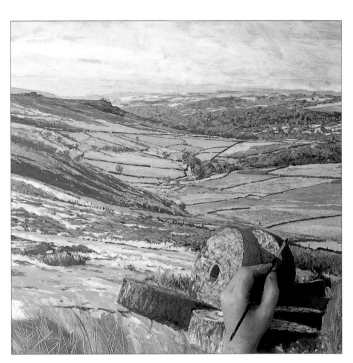

13 Mix a slightly darker green from cadmium yellow and phthalocyanine blue and paint the green grass in the immediate foreground. The use of a darker tone pulls this area forwards and makes it seem closer to the viewer. The shaded sides of the millstones look too red in tone and jump forwards too much. Mix a neutral brownish grey from cadmium yellow, cadmium red, cobalt blue and titanium white and paint over these areas, reinforcing the cast shadows with a slightly darker version of the same mixture.

14 Using a very small round brush, paint a thin line of titanium white around the top edge of the millstone that is lying on its side, so that it appears to be rim-lit by the sun.

15 Using a small round brush, drybrush thin strokes of burnt umber over the foreground to the left of the millstones to add texture and create grass stems blowing in the breeze.

The finished painting

Finally, put in the sky using a bright blue mixed from cerulean blue and titanium white. This tranquil landscape simply glows with sunlight and warmth. The scene covers a wide area but the millstones in the foreground, which are positioned slightly off centre, provide a strong triangular shape at the base of

the image and a much-needed focal point. Although they occupy only a small part of the frame, the buildings in the middle distance provide a secondary point of interest, to which our eye is drawn by the gently sloping diagonal lines of the hills and fields.

Strong textures in the foreground help to pull this area forwards and imply that it is closer to the viewer.

The sloping line of the hills leads our eye down towards the buildings, which form a secondary point of interest.

The greens and browns of the fields are modified by the underlying yellow, adding warmth to these rather subdued colours.

Painting still lifes

One of the advantages of painting still lifes is that all the elements are under your control: you don't have to worry about the weather or the light, your subject won't get up and walk away, and potential subjects are all around you in the form of everyday household objects. Nonetheless, planning your composition and making preliminary sketches to check you've got the balance right are absolutely vital.

In traditional still lifes there is normally some kind of thematic link between the various objects, although this is by no means essential. But do look for interesting contrasts of shape and texture. If, for example, you are painting fruit in a bowl, all of which are rounded in shape, introduce a tall, vertical element in the form of a vase in the background. Juxtapose the rough-hewn texture of a rustic wooden table with the smooth, shiny surface of glazed pottery, or the soft texture of velvet with the faceted edges of crystal. Such contrasts will add interest to your painting. Odd numbers of objects (three, five or seven) tend to look better than arrangements of even numbers.

Whatever subject you choose, the most common mistake is not to spend enough time arranging the set-up. When you've selected your subjects, move them around until you're happy with the grouping. Even very slight adjustments can have a big impact on the overall composition. Look at how the shapes overlap and at the overall balance of colours. Triangular compositions work well, as they encourage the viewer's eye to move around the picture. Placing all the elements in a straight line is rarely, if ever, successful.

Look at the spaces between the objects, too; they play an important part in the composition. If the objects are too far apart, they will look as if they don't belong together; if they are too close, the composition may look cluttered.

Another common mistake is including too many things: sometimes, as the saying goes, 'less is more'. If your set-up isn't working, try simplifying the composition by taking items away.

Keep the background simple, too. A plain-coloured wall or piece of fabric in an appropriate colour will allow your chosen objects to stand out – but don't leave too much space around the objects or the background will become too dominant.

Finally, remember to experiment with different viewpoints. It's interesting to note how different objects can look when viewed from above or below, rather than at normal eye level, making your paintings look much more dynamic.

Sweet Williams and cherries ▼
The colour of the flowers is echoed in the cherries that are randomly scattered over the table. The plain wood allows the flowers and fruit to stand out, while the diagonal planks lead our eye through the scene.

Tips: Spend time moving objects around and looking at your set-up from different viewpoints before you begin making your preliminary sketches.
• Take time to sketch a number of thumbnails in order to establish the composition.
• Arrange your still lifes on a board of wood so that, once you have set it up, the entire still life can be turned in order to alter the light.
• Try creating still-life set-ups using unusual or strange-looking objects, in order to create tableaux that are exciting and fresh.

Lemons ▼
The simplest arrangements often work best. Here, lemons in an opaque glass bowl form the centrepiece of the image, their colours and shapes offset by the patterned tablecloth. Note that the bowl is not positioned in the centre of the image; there is slightly more space on the right-hand side, which prevents the image from looking bland and static.

The apple basket ▶
In this still life, in contrast to the painting shown above, the wicker basket in which the fruit are placed is highly textured and intricate. A brightly coloured background would distract, but the terracotta flagstones provide the perfect foil for both basket and fruit. The unusual viewpoint (from almost direcly overhead) enhances the feeling that the scene has been captured *en passant*.

Still life with gourds

A still life does not have to be an elaborate scene in the style of the Dutch Old Masters such as Rembrandt: you can set up a scene on a corner of your table with just a few carefully chosen fruits.

Interestingly, one of the gourds in this painting is artificial – but it is virtually impossible to tell which one. Realistic-looking artificial fruits and flowers are readily obtainable from florists and craft stores and it is worth putting together a small collection of things that you can incorporate into your paintings. An added bonus is that they will not wilt or rot while you are in the process of painting them! Seashells, pieces of driftwood, pebbles and pine cones also make interesting subjects that you can pick up for free while out walking, as well as being attractive items to display around the home.

Odd numbers of objects – three, five, or seven – always seem to look more balanced in a composition than even numbers. Spend time over your arrangement: even a slight adjustment to the position of the your chosen subjects can make a substantial difference to the painting. Placing one object behind the others will give your painting more of a sense of depth: putting everything in a straight line almost always looks boring and static.

If you do not feel up to tackling a complicated background but still want to have something behind your main subject, a small piece of fabric is a good choice. Buy remnants from fabric stores in a variety of colours and patterns; they are inexpensive and don't take up much storage space.

Materials
- *2B pencil*
- *300gsm (140lb) rough watercolour paper*
- *Acrylic paints: yellow ochre, cadmium orange, Hooker's green, ultramarine blue, cadmium red, cadmium yellow, Hooker's green deep hue, titanium white, burnt sienna*
- *Brushes: wash brush, medium round brush that holds a good point*
- *Ruling drawing pen*
- *Masking fluid*
- *Paper towel*
- *Plastic painting knife*

The set-up
Before you start painting, spend time arranging the subjects you have selected for your still life and experiment with different arrangements and viewpoints until you find one that you are happy with: many amateur artists make the mistake of rushing this stage. Here, the gourds have been arranged to create interesting contrasts of scale, colour and texture. Not surprisingly, groups of three objects seem to work well in compositions that are roughly triangular in shape – and if you draw imaginary lines from the tip of the largest gourd down to the base of each of the two foreground gourds, you will see that this is what the artist has done here. The triangular shape of the composition is echoed in the way that she has chosen to drape the background fabric.

1 Using a 2B pencil, lightly sketch the still-life set-up. Put in some of the striations on the surface of the gourds, as the direction of the lines helps to show the curve of the fruits. Using a ruling drawing pen, apply masking fluid over the light-coloured patterns on the background fabric. Look at where the lines of the pattern break, as this indicates the drape of the fabric. Apply a little masking fluid over the dried cow parsley heads in the foreground, and allow it to dry completely.

2 Using a medium wash brush, wet the paper completely with clean water. Mix a pale wash of yellow ochre and brush it over the whole paper, scrubbing on cadmium orange, wet into wet, for the folds of the fabric and the gourds.

3 Mix a dark green from Hooker's green, yellow ochre and a little ultramarine blue. While the first wash is still slightly damp, start putting in the green of the background fabric around the gourds, using broad, confident brushstrokes.

4 Continue painting the green of the background fabric, leaving the underlying yellowy orange wash showing through for the lighter parts of the fabric.

▶

5 Mix a bright orangey red from cadmium red and a little cadmium orange. Using a medium round brush, start painting the red pattern on the fabric and some of the shadows in the background.

6 Mix a dark blue from ultramarine blue with a little Hooker's green and paint the blue pattern on the background fabric. Work quickly, with flowing brush strokes: getting the exact pattern is not important, but the curving lines enliven the painting and contrast with the solidity of the gourds in the foreground. Leave to dry.

7 Now that the background is well established, you can turn your attention to the main subject – the gourds. Mix a warm orange from cadmium orange and a little cadmium yellow and brush it over the largest gourd, making sure your brushstrokes follow the striated lines on the fruit's surface. Use the same colour on the top half of the smallest gourd, and stipple yellow ochre on to the rounded gourd, which has a bumpy surface texture.

8 Mix a thick, bluey-green from Hooker's green deep and ultramarine blue and paint the base of the small gourd, working from the base upwards. As you get near the top half, brush on cadmium yellow, dragging the brush to soften the line between the two halves. Rinse the brush thoroughly. While the paint is still wet, drag the tip of the brush over the green half to lift off lines of paint and reveal the underlying yellow wash applied in Step 2.

9 Using the side of the brush, dab Hooker's green and Hooker's green deep over the largest gourd. It is not a uniform, flat colour, and alternating between the two greens helps to show up the texture. Leave broad lines of the underlying orange showing through. Outline the edge of the small foreground gourd in Hooker's green deep, so that it stands out more clearly. Dab off paint in places with a piece of paper towel to create more texture and visual interest.

 Tip: Turn the paper towel around in your hand each time you press it on to the paper so that you are using a clean area and don't accidentally dab paint back on to the support.

10 Mix a thick, warm yellow from cadmium yellow, titanium white and a little cadmium orange and paint the light areas on the rounded gourd in the foreground. Using the tip of the brush, dot on burnt sienna in places to indicate the bumpy surface texture. Mix ultramarine blue with titanium white and paint some of the pale, muted blues in the background fabric; loosely brush burnt sienna on to the right-hand side of the painting, outside the draped background fabric. Leave to dry.

11 Using your fingertips, gently rub off the masking fluid from the cow parsley and the background fabric. Run your fingers over the surface of the painting to make sure you have removed all of the masking fluid.

▶

Assessment time

Take some time to stand back and think about what still must be done.
The shapes, colours and patterns are all established, but the foreground gourd,
in particular, still looks a little flat and needs to stand out more from the
background.

The background
fabric should look
more three-
dimensional.

The areas
protected by the
masking fluid are
distractingly
bright.

The texture of
this gourd is not
as pronounced as
it should be.

12 Mix a dark brown from burnt
sienna and a tiny amount of
Hooker's green deep and brush the
mixture over the heads of cow parsley
in the foreground. Mix cadmium orange
with titanium white and, using the tip
of the brush, "draw" the little florets of
the dried cow parsley heads as criss-
crossing, star-shaped lines. The shapes
do not have to be exact; just aim to
give an impression of the texture. The
colour provides a visual link with
the colours of the gourds and the warm
orangey red of the background fabric.

13 Mix a pale yellow from cadmium yellow and a little
titanium white and brush over the exposed masking
fluid lines on the background fabric. Mix a very pale blue from
ultramarine blue and titanium white and paint flowing lines
on the background fabric, noting how the fabric drapes.

14 Using a plastic painting knife, dot blobs of the pale
yellow mixture used in Step 13 over the surface of the
bumpy gourd in the foreground, where the raised surfaces
catch the light. This enhances the texture of the gourd and
helps to make it look more three-dimensional.

The finished painting

Gourds and other autumn fruit and vegetables make attractive subjects for still lifes. Instead of painting the subject in photorealistic detail, the artist has interpreted the scene loosely, creating an animated painting that is full of swirls of colour and interesting textures. Too precise a rendering of the background fabric, in particular, could have resulted in an overly tight piece of work that lacked any sense of life.

Note the contrast between wet-on-dry paint applications on the fabric and the wet-into-wet blurs of the background.

Specks of warm, bright yellow on the cow parsley help to bring it forwards in the painting.

Dots of thick burnt sienna and pale yellow applied with a painting knife create the textured surface of the gourd.

The yellow lines are created by lifting off wet paint with a damp brush or paper towel to reveal the underlying colour.

Still life with pebbles

This project is all about taking something very mundane and making a painting from it. Although we may tend to think of still lifes as being carefully controlled compositions, in which every element is deliberately placed, potential subjects are all around us. It's simply a matter of keeping your eyes open. In this project, a random arrangement of pebbles and lengths of twine in a small fishing harbour, which the artist came across quite by chance, has been transformed into a colourful painting that is full of texture and interest.

Of course, "found" still lifes still require a certain amount of input on the part of the artist. You have to decide how much of the scene to include, and where to place the edges of the painting. You may even have to move things around a little

to get the effect you want, although beware of doing too much as this can destroy the spontaneous, natural look.

In this project, the pebbles are more or less life-size. Painting a smaller subject than normal is a useful exercise, as you will have to look at things in a different way. If you often paint landscapes, for example, your initial instinct might be to scan the scene rapidly to gain an impression of the key elements; you will probably then spend time working out how best to make these elements stand out. When you concentrate on a small area, as here, every element counts: you need to slow down and look at how the different parts relate to one another in terms of their size, shape and colour, and adjust your position until you are sure you have got the

best viewpoint. At this scale, moving just one step to the left or right, backwards or forwards, can make a real difference.

Materials
- Illustration board
- B pencil
- Gouache paints: cadmium yellow deep, cadmium orange, burnt umber, phthalocyanine blue, ultramarine blue, zinc white, ivory black, cerulean blue, mid green, flame red, lemon yellow
- Brushes: large wash, old toothbrush, small round, fine round
- Rag or absorbent kitchen paper
- Small painting knife
- Acrylic gold size
- Gold leaf

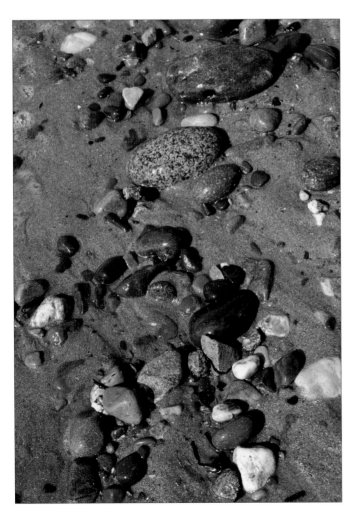

The scene
Pebbles in a harbour, glistening with water left by the retreating tide, present an interesting challenge. When painting a subject like this, look for contrasts of size and colour.

1 Using a B pencil, mark a grid of squares on your paper. Many of the pebbles are similar in size and shape, so the grid will help you to keep track of which pebble you are painting. Again using the B pencil, make a light underdrawing.

2 Mix separate washes of cadmium yellow deep and cadmium orange. Wash cadmium yellow deep over the whole paper. While it is still wet, brush in cadmium orange, leaving some areas as pure yellow. Press a clean rag or absorbent kitchen paper over the top right of the paper, to lift off some of the orange. Leave to dry.

3 Load an old toothbrush with burnt umber and any other colours that you can detect in the sand, and drag a painting knife through the bristles to spatter paint over the paper, creating a background of large-grained sand. (If you don't have a painting knife, an ordinary kitchen knife will work just as well.) Leave to dry.

4 Mix various blues and greys from phthalocyanine blue, ultramarine blue, zinc white and ivory black. Using a small round brush, begin putting in the pebbles. Note that you are simply placing the pebbles at this stage; although they look like flat circles and ovals, you will begin to build up the form later.

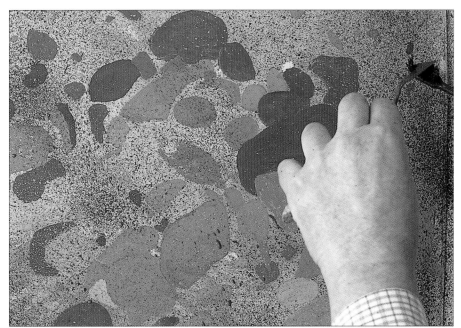

5 Continue putting in the pebbles, varying the colours. Some have a purple undertone; others have a greenish tinge, created from a base colour of mid green plus zinc white or ivory black, as appropriate. Leave to dry.

6 Load the toothbrush with cadmium yellow deep. Drag a painting knife through the bristles, as in Step 3, to spatter both the pebbles and the sand with yellow paint. Repeat the process with flame red and lemon yellow.

Tip: To get the size of the spatters right, try practising on a piece of card, holding the toothbrush at different distances from the painting.

▶

7 While the yellow spattering is still wet, drag a rag or a piece of absorbent kitchen paper over the spatters on some of the larger and darker pebbles to create streaked marks. On other pebbles, simply dab off any excess paint with a damp cloth to reveal the underlying colours, so that the spatters look like mica or other mineral crystals lodged within the stone, rather than lichen growing on top.

Assessment time

The initial blocking in of colours is complete, and the sand (which contains spatters of several different colours) looks convincingly textured, but at this stage the majority of the pebbles simply look like circles or ovals of dark colour positioned within the sand, rather than three-dimensional objects. The lighting is fairly flat and uniform, so there are no clearly defined shadows to help you, but if you look closely you will see differences in both tone and colour temperature, with the sides of the pebbles that are turned away from the light being cooler (bluer) in colour. As you complete the painting, you should concentrate on reinforcing these tonal contrasts and on giving the pebbles more texture.

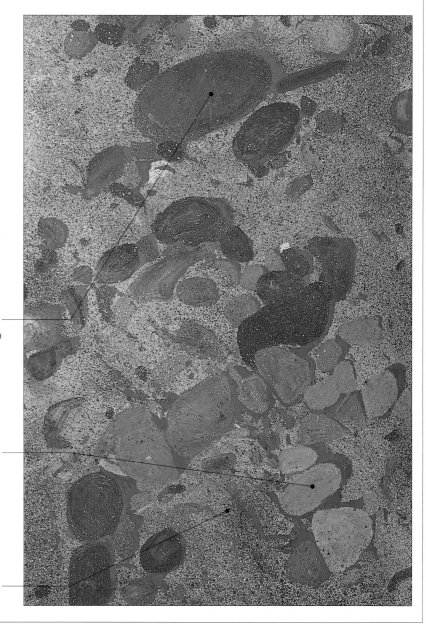

Smudging wet paint over dry has created streaks of paint that provide a good basis on which to build up more texture.

The shape of the pebbles is clear, but so far they all look flat and two-dimensional.

The texture of the sand has been built up well by blending colours wet into wet and by spattering.

8 Mix a bright but chalky blue from cerulean blue and a little zinc white. Using a small round brush, brush this mixture over the brightest parts of any blue-grey pebbles. Mix a pale yellow from cadmium yellow deep, lemon yellow and zinc white, and a pale pink from flame red and white, and dab these mixtures over the large, pale pebble near the top of the painting, using short horizontal brushstrokes. Mix a dilute, neutral shadow colour from phthalocyanine blue and a little burnt umber. Paint the small shadows to the right of the largest pebbles; they immediately look much more three-dimensional.

9 Continue to build up the texture and tonal contrasts within the pebbles, using all the colours on your palette – pale yellows and pinks, blue-greys, and almost pure white for the very lightest pebbles.

10 Vary your brushstrokes, stippling the paint in some places and using short strokes in others, but always allowing some of the underlying colours to show through.

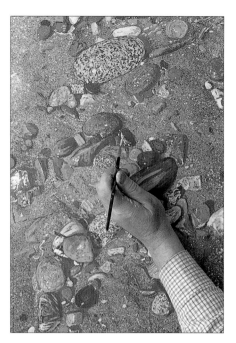

11 Using a very fine brush, stipple all the colours on your palette on to the sand to create the appearance of large grains of sand or very tiny pebbles. Stand back from your work at regular intervals in order to see how the whole painting is progressing.

12 Many different colours have now been spattered and stippled on to the sand, creating a suitably granular-looking background for the pebbles. Take time to assess whether or not the texture of the sand is complete before you move on to the next stage.

13 If some of the stones look too dark in relation to the rest of the image, stipple or dab on some of your very pale yellow mixture. Use artistic licence where necessary in your choice of colours and keep looking at the balance of the painting as a whole.

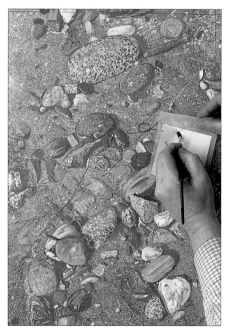

14 Now for the final touch – the twine that twists and turns its way through the pebbles, creating a dynamic diagonal line that draws our eye through the composition. Using a fine round brush, "draw" the line of the twine in acrylic gold size. Leave the size until it is tacky to the touch, following the manufacturer's instructions.

15 Lift a small piece of gold leaf by the backing paper and position it on the sized surface. Brush over the backing paper with a soft brush. Press a piece of kitchen paper over the gold leaf to ensure that it adheres firmly. Brush off any excess gold leaf with a clean, dry brush.

The finished painting

This is a deceptively simple-looking still life, but the gradual build-up of tones and textures makes it very convincing. A number of textural techniques have been used, and the artist has exploited the chalky consistency of gouache paint to give the pebbles solidity. The use of gold leaf for the twine is an imaginative touch that adds yet another texture to the image.

The trick with a painting like this is not to overwork it. Try to build up the image as a whole, rather than trying to finish one small area before you move on to the next. Taking time out at regular intervals, so that you can stand back and assess whether or not you've built up the textures to the degree that you want, is also important.

Just a hint of a shadow under the right-hand edge of the largest pebbles is enough to make them look three-dimensional.

The different facets of the stones have been carefully observed.

The twine, created by applying gold leaf, snakes its way through the image in a diagonal line.

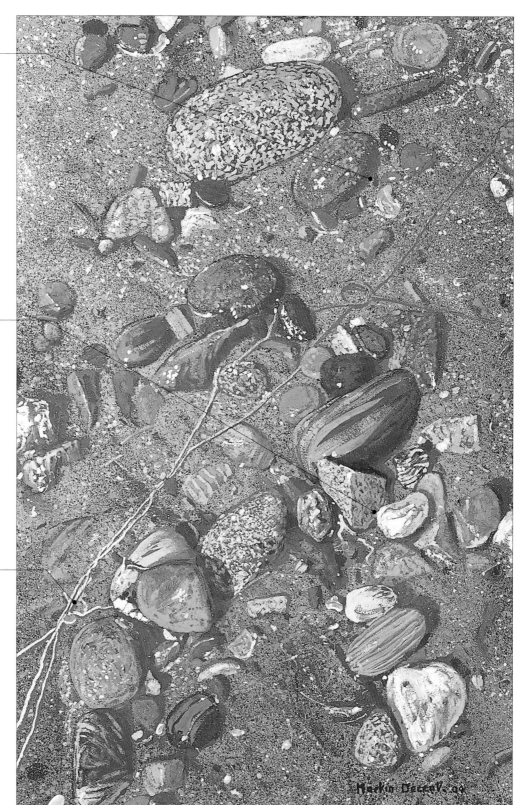

Lemons in glass dish

Less is very often more when painting still lifes; in other words, a small number of objects, carefully arranged, is often more effective than an elaborate set-up of many different elements. What could be simpler than a few lemons in a glass dish?

However, you still need to take time and care over your arrangement. Place the lemons so that they create an attractive overall shape, and look at the balance of the composition and at the spaces between the objects. Does the arrangement look too heavily weighted towards one side? Do the lemons make an interesting shape that draws our eye around the picture? Positioning the lemons at different angles and cutting one of them in half, so that we can see its internal structure, adds interest to the scene.

Because clear glass takes on the colours of the objects around it, you need to establish the background colour and the colour of any objects seen through the glass before you can turn your attention to the glass itself.

The highlights on both the dish and the lemons require careful study, but you should resist the temptation to put in every single one: too many highlights can easily detract from your main subject. Half-close your eyes, as this makes it easier to assess which highlights are the most prominent and therefore the most important.

Shadows are an essential part of the composition, too, with both the lemon on the table top and the glazing bars of the window casting interesting shadows that tell us about the direction and intensity of the light. Beginners sometimes make the mistake of adding black to the local colour of an object to make its shadow colour, but shadows often contain a hint of the complementary colour, as well as colours reflected from nearby objects. Here, for example, the lemon's shadow contains some violet – the complementary of yellow. Even within the shadows there are warm and cool colours and light and dark areas: never paint a shadow as a uniform, flat colour.

Materials
- *Stretched and primed canvas*
- *Oil paints: olive green, lemon yellow, cadmium red, cobalt blue, raw umber, alizarin crimson, titanium white*
- *Turpentine (white spirit)*
- *Brushes: selection of small and medium hogshair*

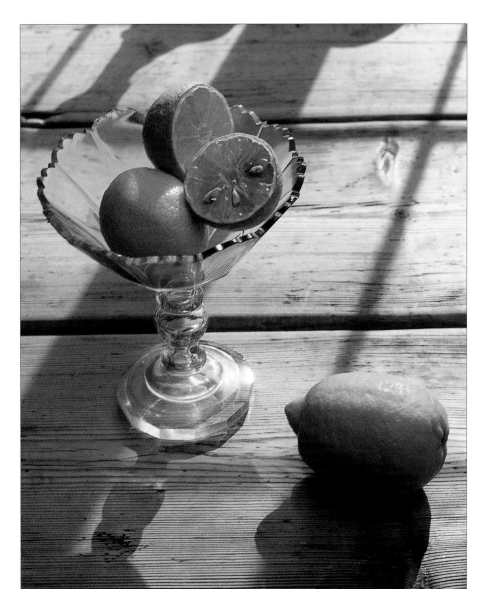

The set-up
Always look for interesting shapes and lines when you're setting up a still life. In this arrangement, the lemons are angled in different directions, which adds interest to the scene. One lemon was also cut in half, which provides the opportunity to explore its internal structure and texture. Although the initial stages of the painting were made in flat lighting conditions, during the second painting session the sun moved round, casting diagonal shadows that form a strong contrast to the horizontal planks of the rough wooden table.

1 Using a small brush and a thin mix of olive green, draw the glass dish. Put in vertical and horizontal guidelines to help you get the shape of the ellipse right and a vertical line as the centre of the stem: these guidelines will be covered up later, but with plain glass it's very obvious if the shape is wrong.

2 Draw the lemons (including the shadow cast by the lemon on the table) and indicate the lines of the planks of wood on the table top. Try to think of the lemons as rounded geometric forms rather than simply drawing an outline, and look at where edges overlap.

3 Once you are happy with your underdrawing, you can start to apply some paint. Mix a dark olive colour from olive green, lemon yellow and a minute amount of cadmium red and block in the shaded sides of the lemons. Add more lemon yellow to your mixture and paint all the unshaded parts of the lemons, including the cut surfaces. Leave unpainted the ring of pith around the edges of the cut lemons.

Tip: Look carefully at the different yellows within the still life; some areas have a blue-green tinge, while others are much warmer. Look at the relative tones, too; you will probably find that the shaded areas are actually much darker than you expected.

4 Block in the shadow under the lemon on the table using a neutral grey mixture of cobalt blue, raw umber and a touch of alizarin crimson. Mix a neutral grey-brown from raw umber, cobalt blue and titanium white. Scumble this mixture over the table top, using diagonal brushstrokes that echo the direction of the light. Note that the colour is not uniform: there are warm and cool areas within it, so adjust the proportions of your mix accordingly.

Tip: Although the scumbling can be fairly loose, take care not to go over the outlines of the lemons or the glass bowl. One advantage of scumbling is that it allows some of the underlying colour to show through, and this helps to create the texture of the rough wooden table top. The contrast between this texture and that of the more smoothly painted glass bowl and lemons will be important in the final painting.

Assessment time

Clear glass has no colour of its own; it takes its colour from what is around it, so you need to establish the basic tonal framework of the scene first. Once you have done this, you can concentrate on refining the lights and dark, and on making the glass really look like glass.

Spend time assessing which colours and tones are reflected in the glass before you apply any more paint.

The lemons are starting to look rounded, but require more work in order to look convincing.

5 Now begin to indicate the different facets of the glass dish by putting in warm (pinky brown) or cool (blue-biased grey) lines as appropriate. Brush a pale blue around the rim of the cut lemons.

Tip: Each facet of the glass is a slightly different tone, as it is angled differently towards the light. Look beyond the glass and see what colours you can see through it to assess these tonal changes.

6 Continue to paint the stem and the base of the glass dish, using warm- or cool-biased mixes as appropriate. The tone can change quite dramatically within a small area, so take your time and use a small brush.

7 Using the same pale blue colour that you used around the rim, lightly touch in the segments on the surfaces of the cut lemons and put in the highlights reflected in the base of the glass dish.

8 Using a pale yellow mixed from lemon yellow and white, draw in the highlights on the foreground lemon. Use slightly uneven, broken strokes to create texture on the surface of the lemon.

▶

9 Now put in the scalloped edge of the dish. The crisp lines of the cut glass pick up highlights, and you can use these to imply the shapes. Use a small brush and put little touches of blue-grey around the back of the dish, which is largely in shadow, and white tinged with yellow around the front.

10 Using a fine sable brush and almost dry paint, gently stroke fine lines of the grey-brown mixture from Step 4 over the table top to imply the grain of the wooden table. The effect is subtle but it adds much-needed texture to the table top without detracting from the still-life arrangement.

11 Mix a pale blue-grey from cobalt blue, titanium white and a little of the mixture used to paint the table top in Step 10. Block in the diagonal shadows cast on the table by the glazing bars in the window, scumbling the mixture on thinly so that some of the underlying colour comes through. Paint the shadow cast by the glass in the same way. This immediately brings more drama to the scene.

Tip: It's very often the contrast between light and dark areas that gives a painting its impact. If the scene doesn't look as strong as you would like, try darkening the dark areas rather than lightening the light ones. If the scene is allowed to become too high-key, the drama may be lost.

The finished painting

The drama of the lighting enhances this little still life immeasurably, with the strong diagonal shadows giving the scene much more drama and impact. The highlights are not overstated but bring much-needed sparkle to the work. A mix of cool and warm tones in the glass provides information about the strength and direction of the light.

The contrast between light and dark areas is what gives the still life its impact.

Both cool and warm tones can be seen in the glass dish.

Relatively thick paint captures the texture of the lemon skin beautifully.

Still life with glass and ceramics

This project is primarily an exercise in observing and painting glass and hard-edged, solid-coloured objects. The technique chosen suits the hard, crisp quality of the objects.

The thing to remember when painting clear glass is that it has no colour of its own: any colour that you can see comes from surrounding objects that are either reflected in the glass or can be seen through it.

Although we know that solid-coloured objects such as the play bricks and pots in this scene are a uniform colour, you cannot paint them as such: their position in relation to the light source means that some areas will be darker or lighter in tone than others, and you must convey these tonal variations in order to make your picture look three-dimensional. There will also be some very bright, almost white, highlights where the lights catches one edge of the object. Although there are relatively few colours in this still life, there is a great deal of tonal variation, which you need to assess very carefully.

Shadows also play an important part in creating a three-dimensional impression. Keep the lighting simple: use just one light, positioned to one side of the objects so that they cast soft shadows both on to other objects within the group and on to the background wall. You can control the size and intensity of the shadows by altering the distance between the light and the objects. If you find that the shadowed side looks too dark, place a sheet of white cardboard or hang a piece of white fabric (a T-shirt will do) on the other side of the still life from the light in order to reflect some light back on to the collection of objects.

Materials
- *MDF (medium density fibreboard) primed with acrylic gesso*
- *B pencil*
- *Acrylic paints: phthalocyanine blue, titanium white, alizarin crimson, burnt umber, yellow ochre, cadmium yellow, phthalocyanine green, purple lake, cadmium red*
- *Matt acrylic medium*
- *Brushes: medium flat*

The set-up
This still life is an eclectic mix of stoneware pots and glass bottles, chosen for the contrast between transparent objects and ones that are solid, and children's play bricks and a wooden ball, selected for their contrasts in shape and colour. Light from a table lamp, positioned out of shot to the right of the set-up, casts interesting shadows on both the objects and the background wall.

1 Using a B pencil, make a light underdrawing of the still life. Include the highlights and shadows, as these are an integral part of the composition.

2 Mix a dull grey from phthalocyanine blue, titanium white, a tiny amount of alizarin crimson, and a few drops of matt acrylic medium, which makes the paint transparent and a little smoother. Using a medium flat brush, block in the shadows of the objects on the background, and the shadow that can be seen through the glass bottle on the left, leaving some of the highlights untouched. Use the same grey to outline the glass bottles, which take their colour from surrounding objects and reflections.

3 Add alizarin crimson and burnt umber to the mixture to make a light brown and start to paint the table, working carefully around the objects but remembering to paint the table that can be seen through the glass bottles.

4 Continue until you have completed the table. Use the same light brown to block in the large, lidded ceramic jar in the background and the bottom part of the stoneware jar on the left.

> **Tip**: The brushmarks will remain evident as the paint dries. Do not try to smooth them out or obliterate them, even though the objects you are painting are smooth in texture, as the brush marks give added interest to the painting.

5 Mix a deep brown from burnt umber, yellow ochre and alizarin crimson and paint the dark rim of the stoneware jar. The flat brush makes it easy to paint straight edges such as this. Use a very thin version of the blue-grey mixture from Step 2 to paint the glass bottle on the right.

6 Mix pale brown from yellow ochre and burnt umber and paint the shaded interior of the foreground jar, leaving the highlit rim untouched. Mix a pale, greyish green from the previous pale brown mixture and a little phthalocyanine blue and paint the lightest areas on the green foreground jar with broad, vertical brushstrokes. Add a little alizarin crimson to the mixture used to paint the inside of the foreground jar and paint the ball in the foreground, leaving the highlights white.

7 Now paint the children's bricks in the foreground, using phthalocyanine blue, cadmium yellow, and a bright green mixed from cadmium yellow and phthalocyanine green. Add some blue to the green mixture and start painting the green jar, working around the dull green highlights that you put down in the previous step.

8 Paint the rim of the green jar, painting around the highlights. Now paint the background. Add more titanium white to the pale brown mixture used in Steps 3 and 4 and brush around the outlines of the objects, feathering the brush strokes upwards, away from the jars. The flat brush makes it easy to work right up to the edge of each object.

Assessment time
The basic shapes and reflections have been put in, and all the objects have been given one layer of colour. You can see, however, that the picture looks rather flat and two-dimensional. You need to work over the whole painting again, increasing the tonal contrasts and adding more detail, in order to make the image look three-dimensional and make the objects stand out clearly from the background.

The large brown pot, in particular, lacks form and merges with both the background and the objects in front of it.

The absence of shadow makes it hard to "read" the image and work out the strength and intensity of the light.

9 Mix a very pale, dilute blue from phthalocyanine blue and titanium white. Paint over the interior of the right-hand glass bottle, working around the highlights and using vertical brushstrokes. Although the glass is clear, it should be slightly darker in tone than the background wall that can be seen through it.

10 Mix a very pale brown from titanium white and burnt umber and fill in the colour in the lower half of the right-hand glass bottle, through which you can see the colour of the wooden table. Mix a rich brown from alizarin crimson, burnt umber and yellow ochre and paint the ball. Add a little purple lake to the mixture and paint the rim of the two-tone stoneware jar.

11 Use the same dark brown for the shadow under the lid of the stoneware jar in the background and on the darkest areas of the lid itself, remembering to paint around the highlights. Darken the tone of both stoneware jars, using vertical brushstrokes and reserving the highlights. Add phthalocyanine blue to the brown mixture and paint the shadow of the glass bottle on the large jar. Use the same colour on the left-hand edge of the bottle, which picks up reflected colour from the green jar to its left.

12 Strengthen the colours on the children's play bricks, making the tones slightly darker on the shaded sides. The shape of the brush will help you to keep the edges of the bricks straight.

▶

13 Paint over the green jar again, using the same paint mixture as in Step 7, again reserving the highlights. The jar is now beginning to take on more depth and solidity.

14 Add burnt umber to the green mixture used in the previous step and, using the edge of the brush, paint a shadow under the base of the green jar, the ball, and the bricks. This has the effect of giving a crisper edge to the objects and helps to define them more clearly. Add alizarin crimson, yellow ochre and a little purple lake to the shadow mixture and paint the deep shadows between the bricks and the jars, and between the ball and the green jar.

Tip: MDF primed with acrylic gesso is perfect for this subject, which consists of smooth-surfaced, hard-edged objects. You could create a softer image by working on canvas or by adding a retarding medium.

15 Mix a purplish blue from phthalocyanine blue, cadmium red and titanium white and reinforce the shadow colour on the wall. Mix a dark, warm brown from phthalocyanine blue, burnt umber and a little cadmium red and darken the shadow under the lid of the stoneware jar. Add more red to the brown mixture and darken the ball.

16 Add phthalocyanine green to the brown mixture to make a very dark green and paint the very dark shadow cast by the ball on the side of the green jar.

The finished painting

All the surfaces in this still life are very smooth and hard, and so an impasto approach, with lots of textured paint, would be inappropriate. Here the artist has built up the layers gradually, adjusting the tones and colours until he achieved the correct density. He has also paid close attention to the shadows and the way the light casts highlights on the objects, as these things are critical in making the objects look three-dimensional.

Glass takes its colour from surrounding objects which are either reflected in it or seen through it; here, colour is reflected from the shadows cast on the background.

The highlights, which are mostly left white, reveal the intensity and the direction of the light source and show up the different facets of the jars.

The shadow cast by the bottle is subtly coloured but helps to make the bottle look more three-dimensional.

Painting buildings

Although you can get away with shapes and proportions being slightly wrong in some subjects (landscapes, for example), if buildings in your paintings are askew, it will be very noticeable. If you are painting anything other than a head-on view of a façade, therefore, you must give some consideration to perspective. This sounds a lot scarier than it is: in fact, a combination of careful observation and a little basic theory, which you can get from any good book on drawing, will set you on the right track. Just remember that all parallel lines on the same plane recede to the same vanishing point.

Unless you are very confident, start by making a light underdrawing and measuring the different parts of the building. Using a pencil to measure things is a classic method that artists have employed for centuries. Hold the pencil out in front of you at arm's length and align the tip with the top of the building. Then run your thumb down the pencil until it aligns with the base. Transfer this measurement to your canvas, again keeping the pencil at arm's length and holding your arm straight. Look, measure and then check again; in fact, whatever you are painting, you should make a conscious effort to spend more time looking at your subject than you do looking at the canvas.

Buildings are one area where including a lot of detail in your underdrawing can really help you, as establishing the relative sizes and positions of doors, windows, arches and other features is critical. Also remember to count: if there are five arched window on a façade, make sure there are also five in your underdrawing.

It is also important to assess the tones in your subject carefully. The exterior of a building is often comprised of one main material (brick, concrete, stucco, for example) and hence it is largely through differences in tone that we make it look three-dimensional. Remember that both acrylic and gouache paints look slightly darker when dry than when wet; test your mixes on scrap paper, and leave them to dry so that you can judge the real tones before you apply them to your painting. Shadows also play a part in this: even a small shadow cast by a window ledge or a decorative embellishment such as a stone statue or door knocker will contribute to the three-dimensional illusion.

Once you have established the basic form of the building, you can put in decorative details and textures. On worn, weathered buildings and peeling paintwork, scumbling is often a good technique for creating texture. If you are painting in acrylic, you might also consider using one of the many proprietary texture mediums on the market. Drybrush, sgrafitto, spattering and sponging are all useful techniques for creating texture on buildings.

◀ **Rouen Cathedral**
This is a scene that has been painted countless times, most notably by the French Impressionist artist Claude Monet (1840–1926). In this version, the plants and café umbrellas bring a touch of modernity to the scene and hint at the bustling street life that goes on around the cathedral.

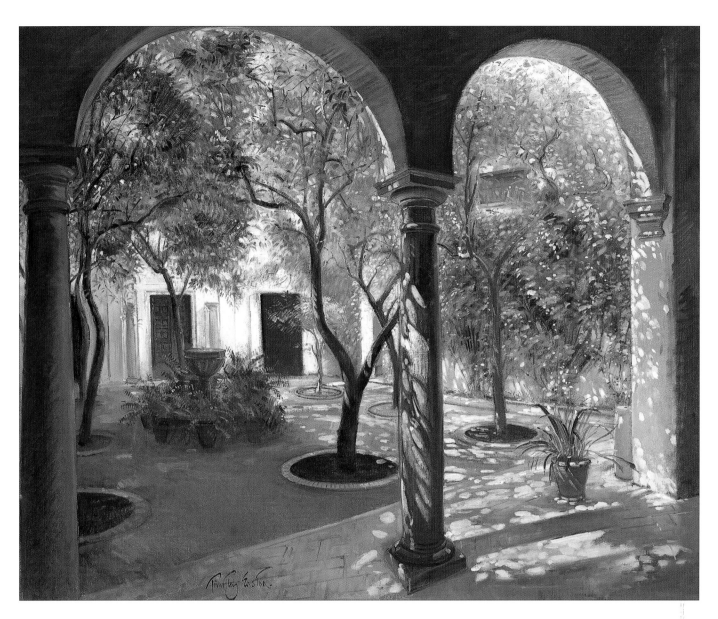

Tips: Observe the rules of perspective and make a light underdrawing to check that you have got things right; this will ensure that your building does not look as if it is about to fall over.
• Draw and paint your building in the same order that it was built – the main structure first, followed by doors and windows, and finally architectural details such as railings and statues.
• If you are painting the façade of a building, pay particular attention to the direction and length of any shadows: they will help you to create a sense of depth in an otherwise flat subject.

The shaded courtyard ▲
This is a delightful evocation of a shaded courtyard in southern Spain. The shadows cast by the plants and the arches create an intriguing and lively pattern of dappled light on the ground. Note that the shadows are predominantly purple in tone: shadows are rarely, if ever, black.

Midday, Gnomon ▶
Textures and the strong diagonal midday shadows are what make this somewhat dilapidated building look so interesting. Scumbles of oil paint allow the underlying colours to show through – a classic method of conveying the texture of worn, weathered surfaces.

Church in snow

Buildings are an integral part of many landscape paintings. Even when they're not necessarily the prime focus of attention, they add an element of human interest by implying the presence of man; and they also help to give a sense of scale.

In this project, the church in the background brings another dimension to a tranquil rural setting. Its solid form, positioned roughly on the third, contrasts well with the landscape around.

Begin by establishing the basic shape of the building and painting it as a flat area of tone. You can then develop this, creating contrasts of light and shade that reveal the different sides of the building, and finally putting in just enough detailing to tell us about the architectural style and period. The human brain is amazingly adept at interpreting a few generalized indications of shape and texture, and too much information can actually destroy the balance of the painting as a whole – particularly when the building is in the background, as here. The further away something is, the less detail is required.

For this project, the artist began by toning the canvas with dilute olive green oil paint. The cool colour suits the wintry scene and gives a good, neutral mid-tone from which to start painting.

Just like water, snow reflects colour from the sky and objects nearby. Where the sun strikes, the snow may be tinged with warm yellows or even pinks, depending on the time of day, while shadows will contain shades of blue and violet. Resist the temptation to paint everything as a brilliant, monotone white: shadowy areas contrasting with small patches of bright, sunlit snow will have far more impact. The shadows in the snow also reveal the contours of the land beneath.

Materials

- *Stretched and primed canvas*
- *Oil paints: olive green, permanent mauve, titanium white, cobalt blue, raw sienna, viridian, burnt sienna, Indian yellow, cadmium red, lemon yellow*
- *Turpentine*
- *Brushes: selection of small and medium filberts*

The scene

Although the church is far away and relatively indistinct, it is still the main focus of the scene. Along with the trees, it provides a strong vertical element on which the viewer's eye can alight, while the curve of the water leads us around the scene.

1 Make an underdrawing of the church, main trees and water area, using a small brush and thin olive green paint. When you paint buildings it is particularly important to get the proportions and angles right, so measure carefully and take your time over this stage. Also indicate the shadows on the snow in the foreground and roughly scumble in the largest reflections in the water.

2 Block in the trees on the far bank, using a mid-toned purple mixed from permanent mauve, titanium white, cobalt blue and raw sienna, and a blue-green mixed from olive green, viridian and a tiny amount of burnt sienna. Using a small brush, begin putting in the cool shadows on the snow on the far bank, using a blue-grey mixed from cobalt blue, titanium white and permanent mauve.

3 Continue putting in the shadows on the snow on the far side of the water. Block in the reflections of the trees in the water, using olive green for the darkest trees and lighter olive green and purple mixes elsewhere, and leaving gaps for the brightest areas of water.

4 Mix a pinkish brown from burnt sienna, titanium white and cobalt blue and paint the walls of the church. Paint the snow-covered roof, which is in shadow, in a cool blue-grey. Overlay some pale blue on the purple trees in the background; this helps to link the trees with the snow.

Assessment time
Lively scumbles are a quick way of establishing basic shapes and tones in the early stages of a painting, and are particularly useful when you are painting outdoors. The underpainting is now virtually complete. For the rest of the painting, concentrate on texture and detailing, checking periodically to ensure that you maintain the tonal balance.

The church, which has been roughly blocked in, adds solidity to the scene.

Lively scumbles establish the basic shapes and tones.

5 Indicate the grasses on the near bank by scumbling on a little of the dark green mixture from the previous step and raw sienna. The warmth of the raw sienna helps to bring them forward in the painting. Brush on more blue for the shadows in the foreground snow, using horizontal strokes that follow the direction of the shadows. For the unshaded areas of snow, use a warm off-white colour mixed from titanium white and a tiny amount of Indian yellow.

6 Using a fine brush and the purplish-grey mixture from Step 2, put in the bare branches that poke up from the ivy-covered trees in the background. Don't try to put in every single detail or the painting will start to look overworked and fussy; you can create a general impression of the shape and texture of these thin branches by means of a series of short parallel lines. Reserve the main detailing and texture for the foreground of the scene.

7 Put in the thin saplings along the bank, as well as their reflections. Darken and strengthen the colours of the reflections: once you've established the general area, you can smooth out the brushstrokes, blending the colours together on the canvas.

8 There is an overly bright and distracting area of water near the centre of the image, which needs to be toned down in order to blend in with the rest of the painting. Leaving the brightest areas untouched, lightly brush a very pale purple over this area.

9 Mix a warm but pale yellow from Indian yellow and titanium white. Lightly touch it into the sky, where the winter sun shines through from behind the clouds.

10 Continue with the linear, drybrush detailing on the bare branches of the trees, as in Step 6, again resisting the temptation to put in too much detail.

11 Using a fine sable brush and a pale blue-grey mixture, put in the branches of the young saplings on the bank. Adjust the proportions of the colours in your mixture: the shaded branches are bluer in tone, while those branches to which the snow is clinging are whiter.

Tip: If the marks look too sharp, soften them by blending them with your fingers.

12 Strengthen the colours of the low bushes on the far side of the water, using short vertical strokes of reddish browns and dark olive greens. The warm colours help to bring this area forwards in the painting.

▶

13 Using thin paint, draw the shapes of the box topiary and geese on the near bank. Roughly block in the shapes of the topiary with a pale blue-green mixture, adding more white on the side that catches the light. Using the same colours as before, brush in the shadows cast by the topiary and the geese.

14 Warm up the foreground snow by scumbling the off-white colour from Step 5 over those areas that are not in shadow. Paint the geese in a blue-tinged white, adding more blue to the mixture for the markings on the feathers. Paint their feet, legs and beaks in cadmium red mixed with white and a little lemon yellow.

15 Using a paler version of the stone colour from Step 4, paint the sunlit sides of the church so that the building looks three-dimensional. Paint the lines on the tower in a blue-grey, adding more white where the snow clings to the ridges. Paint the castellations on the turret by overpainting some of the sky colour. Use the brush handle to blend colours around the edge of the church and create a crisp outline.

16 Paint the windows of the church in a dark brown, leaving the underlying colour showing through for the stonework.

The finished painting

This is a muted scene that nonetheless captures the feeling of thin, early-morning winter sunlight very well through its use of pale blues and pinks. The church is rendered indistinctly and almost appears to be seen through a haze, but there is enough detail to tell us about the architectural style. The geese in the foreground are painted in more detail and add life to what might otherwise be a rather static scene. Note how many different tones there are within the snow.

The brushstrokes in the reflections have been softly blended.

Warm but pale yellow in the sky lightens the scene.

The geese and their shadows enliven the foreground.

Arch and balcony

In the eighteenth and early nineteenth centuries, it was common practice for members of the aristocracy to undertake a grand tour of the major cities of Europe in order to complete their education. In those days before the advent of picture postcards and easy-to-use cameras, sketches made *in situ* were, for many, the only means of recording the wonders that they saw. As a consequence, watercolour paintings abound of the sites that they visited: great palaces and chateaux, romantic vistas and ruined follies were all captured on paper to show to admiring friends and relations.

In some respects this project, which relies on careful observation and measuring to record the detail of the building, is very much in the same tradition. However, it also goes beyond that, seeking as it does to capture the spirit of the place and the quality of the light. Attempting to create a sense of atmosphere is one of the things that will lift your work above the level of a technical exercise and turn it into a painting. Moreover, whether you are painting close to home or in a land far away, the very act of consciously examining your subject over an extended period of time somehow seems to imprint the scene in your memory in a way that taking a photograph can never do.

The building that features in this project is the Royal Pavilion, in Brighton, in the south of England, commissioned and closely overseen by the then Prince Regent (later King George IV), who confessed that he cried for joy when he contemplated the Pavilion's splendours.

Often when you are painting buildings – particularly ones such as this, which are rendered in stucco or plaster or constructed from smooth stone – you are dealing with very subtle differences in tone. You need to observe your subject and assess the tonal differences very carefully, as this is what conveys the three-dimensional nature of the building.

Remember, too, that gouache paint always looks slightly darker when it is dry than it does when it is wet. Make sure you test your mixtures on a scrap piece of paper or board and allow them to dry thoroughly before you apply them to your painting, as this is the only way to judge whether or not you have got the mix right. Although it is possible to paint over areas if you find you've made them too dark, it is far better to get the tone right first time – particularly when you are using the gouache in the form of thin washes, as here – otherwise your painting may start to look heavy and overworked.

The scene

Many people might have been tempted to select a viewpoint that included the whole of the arch and window, with the arch symmetrically positioned, but this could lead to a very static composition. This viewpoint is much more interesting: it allows us to see the form of the arch, rather than just a flat façade, while the turret on the edge of the balcony is positioned "on the third".

Materials
- *Watercolour paper*
- *Acrylic gesso*
- *HB pencil*
- *Illustration board*
- *Gouache paints: raw umber, zinc white, jet black, ultramarine blue, brilliant yellow*
- *Brushes: small round*

1 Using a sharp HB pencil, make an underdrawing on watercolour paper primed with acrylic gesso. It is important to measure everything carefully. Pay particular attention to the shape, size and number of the quatrefoil shapes in the tracery of the limestone balcony.

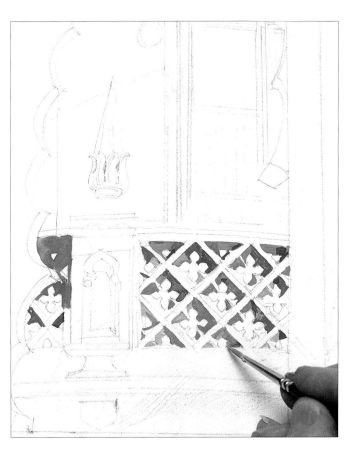

2 Mix a dark brown from raw umber, zinc white and jet black and, using a small round brush, paint the dark spaces around the quatrefoil shapes on the balcony. In some areas light is reflected back: paint these shapes in a blue-grey mixture of zinc white and ultramarine blue.

3 Using the dark brown mixture from Step 2, paint the shaded side of the foreground arch. Add more white to the mixture and paint the dark cast shadows on the right-hand side of the scene, making sure you paint them with crisp edges.

4 Paying careful attention to where the light falls and alternating between the brown and blue-grey mixtures used in the previous steps, paint the scallop shapes on the left-hand side of the foreground arch.

▶

5 Mix a warm stone colour from zinc white, brilliant yellow and a litle raw umber and paint the lightest area of wall behind the balcony. Add ultramarine blue to the dark brown mixture and paint the shaded area above the turret and the edge of the stuccowork to the left of the window.

6 Paint the shaded left-hand side of the foreground arch, using the same dark mixtures as before. Although bright highlights are visible through gaps in the stonework, it is too difficult to try to work around them at this stage: you can reinstate them later using pure white gouache.

7 The blue sky reflected in the window can be seen behind some of the cut-out shapes in the balcony: paint these in a bright blue mixed from ultramarine blue and zinc white. Complete the dark shadows behind the quatrefoil shapes on the balcony; note that the colour changes should not be uniform in tone.

8 Mix a light brown shadow colour from raw umber and zinc white and paint the unpainted stonework on the right of the foreground arch. Scumble a little ultramarine blue over the cast shadows that you painted in Step 3 to make the colour look less flat and create some variety of tone.

9 Add ultramarine blue to the warm stone colour that you mixed in Step 5 and paint the shadow areas on the balcony. Paint the lightest areas of stone on the balcony in a pale mixture of brilliant yellow and zinc white; you will need to look very carefully to see where the tone changes.

10 Add raw umber to the stone colour and paint the area under the overhang of the balcony, which is in shadow and therefore darker in tone. Using a mid-tone brown, put in some of the dark detailing and the most deeply shaded side of the turret.

11 Put in the mid-toned areas of the glazing bars on the window, using a slightly paler version of the stone colour used earlier. Mix ultramarine blue, zinc white and a tiny amount of yellow and paint the reflections of the sky in the window, painting around the very lightest areas, where the curtain hangs in folds.

Tip: To avoid dirtying the white on your palette when mixing it with other colours, use a clean brush and add white to the colour you have already mixed rather than vice versa.

▶

Assessment time

Now that the painting is almost complete, spend some time assessing the tonal values. Is the difference in tone between the light and dark areas strong enough? Any adjustments that you make in the final stages will be very slight.

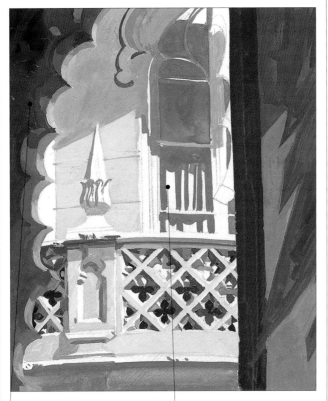

This dark mass tends to overpower the image; the highlights should be reinstated.

The unpainted white areas are too stark; they leap out from the image and demand attention.

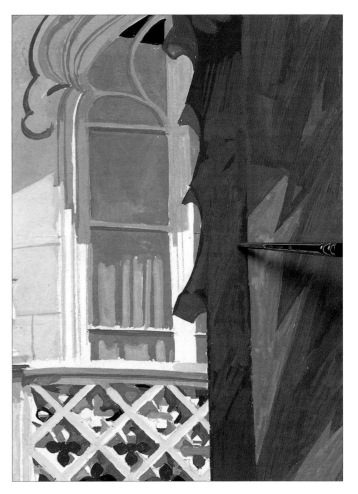

12 Using the stone colour, reinforce the shadows on the underside of the glazing bars. Mix a pale blue from ultramarine blue and lots of zinc white and paint those highlight areas of the curtain that are unpainted. Paint the scalloped edges that jut out from the right-hand side of the arch and scumble a little blue over the darkest part of the arch in order to create some texture and variety of tone in the stonework.

13 Dot in some pure white highlights on the left-hand side of the arch, where light shines through the tracery of the stonework.

Tip: Keep the paint mix quite thick when you are putting in highlights. If you use very watery paint, it is harder to control and may run. Touch the tip of a fine brush into the paint so that there is very little paint on the fibres, and hold the brush almost vertical to the support so that you can make very small, tightly controlled marks.

The finished painting
This is a considered painting of an interesting architectural detail. However the bold shadows and sense of light and shade lift it beyond being a mere record of the building. The arch frames the view, but the fact that it is off-centre creates a more dynamic and interesting composition. The colour palette is limited, but the subtle differences in tone have been carefully observed to create a scene that really looks three-dimensional.

Using gouache enables you to paint highlights over dark paint without any of the underlying colour showing through.

Note how the subtle differences in tone convey the feeling of strong sunlight and the form of the turret.

Scumbling different colours over the darkest area prevents it from looking flat and creates texture and variety in the stonework.

Moorish palace

Small details can often sum up the character of a building far more effectively than a view of the building in its entirety – particularly when, as here, there is an abundance of decorative detail in the form of beautifully shaped arches and mosaic tilework.

This scene shows part of a fourteenth-century Moorish palace in Andalucia, in southern Spain. The view is painted from the central courtyard, which is surrounded by a cool, shaded gallery of the horseshoe-shaped arches that are so typical of this area and period. An arched doorway on one side of the gallery leads into a beautiful walled garden resplendent with splashing fountains.

Try to respect the architect's intentions when you are painting buildings of any kind. Symmetry was an important consideration in Moorish architecture and a symmetrical composition will help you to capture something of the formality of this particular building. Remember, however, that you are making a painting, not an architectural plan: you also have to take into consideration things like the play of light and shade and the contrast between the heat of the garden and the coolness of the gallery.

Materials
- *Acrylic paper*
- *Acrylic paints: phthalocyanine green, phthalocyanine blue, cadmium red, titanium white, lemon yellow, alizarin crimson, ultramarine blue, brilliant yellow green*
- *Brushes: large round, medium flat, medium round, small flat*
- *Charcoal pencil*

The courtyard and gallery
From this angle, the arch creates a "frame within a frame", leading us through to the garden and fountains. We can also see the gallery surrounding the courtyard, which tells us more about the building as a whole, and there is an interesting and atmospheric contrast between the brightly lit garden and the cool, shaded gallery.

The garden and fountains
Here, you can see the garden and fountains clearly. Architecturally, however, it is not as interesting as the view from the courtyard.

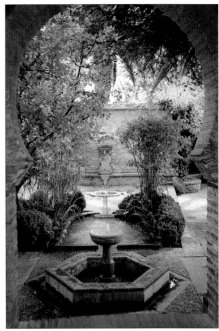

Tip: Always spend time exploring your subject from different viewpoints before you start painting; even a slight adjustment to your position can make a substantial difference. Instead of trying to capture the whole scene, decide what elements appeal to you most – and make quick compositional sketches to decide which viewpoint works best.

1 Mix a bright blue from phthalocyanine green and phthalocyanine blue. Using a large round brush, lay a flat wash over the paper. Leave to dry. Using a charcoal pencil, sketch the scene, observing the perspective carefully to ensure that all the lines run at the correct angles.

2 Mix a warm, off-white stone colour from cadmium red, titanium white and lemon yellow. Using a medium flat brush, paint the lightest tones of the vertical columns and foreground arch. Add a little more red to the mixture and paint the arch into the garden and the line of bricks above the foreground arch.

3 Add more water to the mixture and paint the shaded tiled area of floor beyond the arch. Because the paint is very dilute, it serves as a glaze, allowing some of the colour of the support to show through.

4 Mix a purple shadow colour from alizarin crimson, ultramarine blue and a little lemon yellow and, using a medium round brush, paint the huge wooden doors on each side of the arch leading into the garden. Use a dilute version of the same colour for the tiled courtyard floor.

5 Mix a pale, bright green from brilliant yellow green and titanium white and paint the lightest foliage. Add more brilliant yellow green and a little ultramarine blue and dot in some darker foliage. Paint the pool surround in the stone colour from Step 2, adding more white for the side in sunlight.

▶

6 Mix a warmer stone colour from cadmium red, lemon yellow and titanium white and, using a small flat brush, paint the darker-toned bricks that run around the top of the arch.

7 Paint the fountain base in the same colour and the interior of the fountain bowl in the initial pale stone colour. Add more water to the pale stone colour and scumble it loosely over the ground inside the archway. Reinforce the shadows at the top and base of the supporting columns. Brush a little very dilute lemon yellow over the wooden doors.

Assessment time

Although the dark wooden doors give some indication of perspective and distance, the image looks very flat and two-dimensional. There is some detailing on the brickwork of the arches, but the garden in the background consists of little more than a few blocks of colour. The next stage is to reinforce the sense of depth. More foreground details, suggesting the intricacy of the carved arches, would help to bring the arches forwards in the scene. Introducing some reflected light into the glazed tiles of the gallery floor would help to connect this area with the sunlit garden that lies beyond.

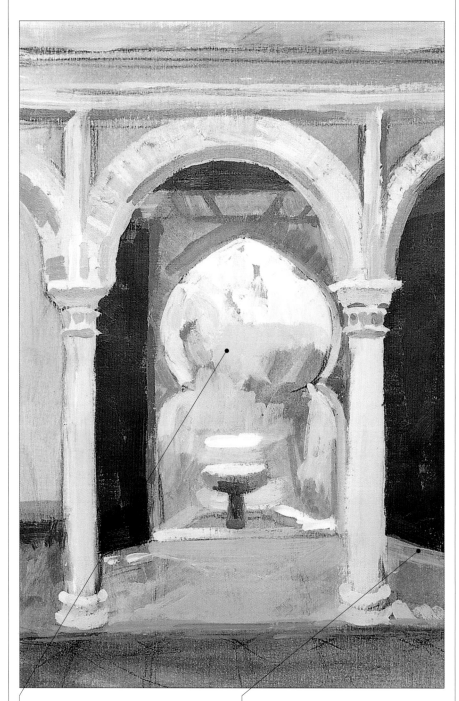

Indistinct masses of green imply the garden beyond, but more definition is needed.

The sloping line of the door gives some indication of depth and perspective.

8 Mix a dark green from phthalocyanine green and brilliant yellow green, and a lighter green from brilliant yellow green and lemon yellow. Using a small round brush, dot these two mixtures over the foliage to give it more form, using the lighter colour higher up, where the sun catches the trees.

9 Mix a dull red from cadmium red, titanium white and a little phthalocyanine blue. Using a medium flat brush, put in the terracotta tiles of the courtyard, leaving lines of the blue glaze showing through. Darken the shaded edge of the step leading into the garden with the same colour.

10 Mix a greenish black from phthalocyanine green and a little ultramarine blue. Block in the dark leaves of the potted plant to the left of the foreground arch and dot the same colour into the foliage in the garden; again, this helps to link the inner and outer courtyards.

11 Add a little cadmium red and some titanium white to the pale stone colour and, using a small flat brush, put in the pink-coloured tiles around the top of the archway. Paint the small blue tiles in this area in a mixture of phthalocyanine blue and titanium white. Darken the shaded edge of the step.

▶

12 Add a little titanium white to the pale stone colour and, using the tip of a small flat brush, paint mortar lines around the top of the arch. Using the same colour, paint the highlit side of the column that separates the central arch from its neighbour.

13 Using a small round brush and the terracotta mixture from Step 9, paint the plaster above the tiles. Paint the decorative tiles above the arch using the same colour and phthalocyanine blue. Interpret the pattern loosely. Add the mortar lines that separate the tiles, as you did in Step 12.

14 Paint the water splashing from the fountain in titanium white. Mix a pale ochre from lemon yellow and brilliant yellow green and paint the back wall of the garden, allowing some of the foliage colour to remain visible.

15 Mix a very dilute, dull purple from alizarin crimson and phthalocyanine blue and paint the shadows cast by the heavy wooden doors on the tiled floor with smooth, even brush strokes.

The finished painting

This painting is all about contrasts: contrasts of light and shade and of warmth and coolness. The colour palette is beautifully balanced: the colour of the blue-toned ground is picked up in the tilework and the water, while terracotta and ochre complement the blue and bring added warmth to the scene. The arch in the foreground acts as a frame for the arched doorway and the garden beyond – an established compositional device that draws the viewer's eye through the picture.

The soft colours of the tiles, brickwork and plaster look faded, as befits the age of the building.

Pale yellows and greens are used to show how strongly the sunlight is hitting the tops of the trees.

The splashing water of the fountain is painted with energetic, curving brushstrokes.

The original blue-toned ground shows through the thin terracotta glaze, creating a feeling of coolness in this shaded area.

Wisteria-covered archway

Using an archway as a frame for a view is a classic compositional device, drawing the viewer's eye through the scene to linger on what lies beyond. Here, however, the view through the arch is little more than a soft, out-of-focus blur: the main interest lies around the arch itself, in the form of the old and somewhat worn brick wall and the violet-coloured wisteria flowers that cascade over it.

In this project, acrylic paint is used both in thin glazes to build up the colour and more thickly, mixed with white, for the mortar lines in the brickwork and the wisteria flowers.

Contrasts of texture are important in building up the image, and a range of techniques is used to achieve this. Spatters of paint in the foreground convey the gravelly texture of the path; fine texture paste on the wall gives a sense of the worn, crumbling brickwork; and different brushstrokes, from flowing curves to short dabs and dashes, capture the textures and shapes of the foreground plants.

Materials
- *300gsm (140lb) NOT watercolour paper*
- *HB pencil*
- *Painting knife*
- *Fine texture paste*
- *Ruling drawing pen or fine-nibbed steel dip pen*
- *Masking fluid (frisket)*
- *Acrylic paints: light blue violet, vermilion, Hooker's green, yellow ochre, titanium white, violet, burnt sienna, cadmium orange, cadmium yellow, ultramarine blue*
- *Brushes: medium chisel or round*
- *Waterproof sepia ink*

The scene
Although this viewpoint shows the arch and pathway well, there is no real focus of interest and the detail of the flowers is indistinct.

The wisteria flowers
By moving around to the right, the artist was able to see more clearly the colours in the petals and how the flowers hang in clusters. Taking reference photographs or making quick sketches of details such as this will prove invaluable.

1 Using an HB pencil, lightly sketch the scene. Using the tip of a small painting knife, dab texture paste randomly over the brickwork and the path. Leave to dry. Dip a ruling drawing pen or fine-nibbed steel dip pen in masking fluid (frisket) and mask out the lightest parts of the wisteria and the other foreground flowers, and the mortar lines around the archway and in the brick wall. Leave to dry.

2 Mix a very dilute wash of light blue violet and, using a medium chisel or round brush, apply it over the sliver of sky that is visible at the top of the image and through the archway. Brush dilute Hooker's green over the foliage that can be seen through the arch. Mix yellow ochre with a little vermilion and titatnium white and brush this mixture over the path on the far side of the arch.

3 Mix separate washes of violet and light blue violet. Alternating between the mixtures, brush these colours over the flowers. For the deepest-coloured flowers, drop more violet, wet into wet, into the first wash. Leave to dry.

4 Brush a dilute wash of burnt sienna over the brick wall, changing to very pale yellow ochre for the lower part of the wall, and a mixture of burnt sienna and cadmium orange over the archway.

▶

5 Mix a warm brown from burnt sienna, Hooker's green and vermilion and, while the brickwork is still wet, drop this mixture into it in places to deepen the colour. Brush in the general shapes of the wisteria foliage and the foliage above the wall in Hooker's green. Using various mixtures of Hooker's green and Hooker's green plus cadmium yellow, start painting the spiky foliage of the foreground plants.

> **Tip**: When painting the foliage, match your brushstrokes to the shape of the plant – curving, calligraphic strokes for long-leaved plants, short dots and dashes for round-leaved plants.

6 Brush the warm brown colour from Step 5 over the foreground and the darkest parts of the wall to build up the colour. While it is still wet, add more burnt sienna to the mixture and spatter it over the first brown. Mix a dark blue-green from Hooker's green and ultramarine blue and paint the foliage to the left of the arch, adding cadmium yellow to the mixture for the grass at the base of the image. Leave to dry.

7 Using the blue-green mixture from the previous step, continue painting the foliage to the left of the arch, noting the spiky shapes of the leaves. Mix a dark brown from violet and burnt sienna and brush this mixture over the wall and path, so that the colour is gradually built up in thin glazes. Apply the colour unevenly to create some tonal variation and texture.

8 Using a technical drawing pen or fine-nibbed steel dip pen loaded with waterproof sepia ink, draw the wrought-iron gateway. (Black ink would look too harsh: sepia is a much more gentle colour.)

Tip: The ink must be waterproof, otherwise it will smudge if any paint is applied on top of it.

9 The wisteria flowers look a little flat; build them up by brushing on pure violet in the darkest areas. Leave to dry.

Assessment time

Rub off the masking fluid with your fingertips; sometimes it is hard to see whether or not you have removed all the fluid, so run your fingers over the whole painting to make sure no lumps of fluid are left. Blow or shake off any loose, dried fluid before you continue painting.

Although the painting is nearing completion, it needs a little more "punch" and contrast. Take some time at this stage to assess where more work is needed: by glazing selected areas with thin layers of acrylic paint, you can build up the colours to the required density while at the same time adding much-needed texture on areas such as the path and brickwork. The adjustments that you make in these final stages of the painting will be relatively small, but they make an important contribution to the overall effect.

The areas previously covered by the masking fluid are too stark and need to be knocked back.

More detail is required in the foreground foliage.

10 Apply a thin glaze of light blue violet over the exposed parts of the wisteria flowers. Mix a dilute yellowy green from Hooker's green and cadmium yellow and brush it over the wisteria trunk and the foliage at the base of the right-hand wall. Mix a blue-green from ultramarine blue and Hooker's green and brush it over the plants to the left of the gate to tint the exposed areas and deepen the foliage colour.

11 Mix a pale, yellowish brown from yellow ochre and green and paint some of the exposed mortar lines in the brickwork. Do not worry if you go outside the mortar lines as it will simply serve as a glaze, enhancing the texture of the crumbling brickwork. Dot violet paint into the wisteria flowers to give more contrast between the light and dark flowers. Paint the shaded interior of the arch in the same colour.

12 Dotting the paint on the tip of the brush, paint the lightest wisteria flowers in a pale, opaque mixture of white and light blue violet. This points up the contrast between the lightest and darkest areas and gives the flowers more depth.

The finished painting
This is a soft, romantic painting of part of an old walled garden. The plants are painted in a fairly loose, impressionistic way rather than as highly resolved botanical studies, but they are nonetheless recognizable from their general shapes and colours. The path draws our eye through the scene to the flower-covered wall and archway; the arch itself is positioned slightly off centre, which adds interest to the composition and prevents it from looking too static.

The blue-green colour of the plants in this area balances the blues and violets of the wisteria.

Although no detail is visible, the garden beyond the archway is implied through the use of soft, muted colours.

The artist has paid careful attention to the different colours within the flowers and to the overall shapes of the flower clusters.

Domestic interior

For this project the artist painted part of his kitchen, with one of his own paintings hanging on the wall. Why not set yourself the challenge of painting a small corner of your own home? It will have relevance and personal associations for you and your family – and you will have the advantage of painting something that you know well already. You can include objects that have special significance for you, such as family heirlooms or holiday souvenirs – but be selective and don't try to include too much, or it will be difficult to establish a centre of interest in the scene.

Choose your viewpoint carefully and remember that it's perfectly all right not to include the whole of an object. Here, for example, the artist decided to include less than half of the table, but did add a tablecloth. This gives an air of informality to the scene, making it seem like a snapshot of family life. The fact that the table is slightly angled, rather than painted square on, also leads the viewer's eye into the scene and makes for a much more dynamic composition.

One of the beauties of working with acrylics is that you can build up several layers of thin glazes. This gives a richness and luminosity to the work, as glazed colours reflect light more readily than opaque colours. This is the approach that is taken in this project and it seems to work particularly well in a scene such as this, which contains many smooth surfaces.

Materials
- *Canvas primed with acrylic gesso*
- *Acrylic paints: cadmium yellow light, raw umber, ultramarine blue, yellow ochre, permanent violet, vermillion, magenta, titanium white, cerulean blue, cadmium red, cadmium yellow deep*
- *Brushes: medium flat, flat wash, small round*
- *Rag*
- *Painting knife*

1 Dot cadmium yellow light acrylic paint over the canvas and wipe over it with a rag to spread the paint over the support. It's better if the coverage is slightly uneven. Leave to dry.

The scene
Fruit and flowers on the table inject colour into a scene that consists largely of wood and brick. The flowers also provide a visual link with the painting on the wall.

2 Using a medium flat brush, "draw" the frame of the painting on the wall and the fireplace recess in raw umber. Mix a dark green from cadmium yellow light and ultramarine blue and outline the struts of the chair, the panels in the dresser and the flower stems. Leave to dry.

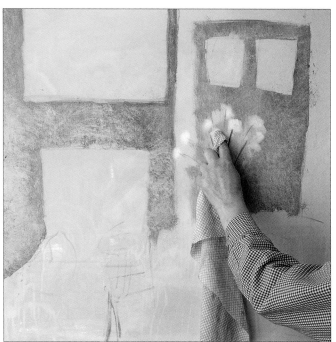

3 Block in the brick-covered chimney breast and the wood of the dresser in yellow ochre, painting around the green flower stems. While the paint is still wet, wet a rag with water and wipe off circular smudges of colour for the flower heads. Although the paint feels dry, it won't be totally immovable for about 24 hours and the yellow will come off if you rub gently.

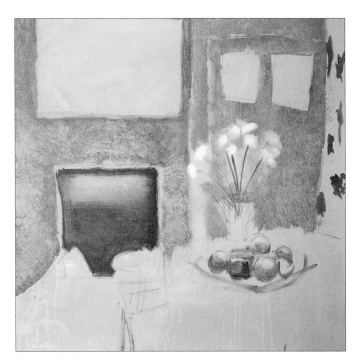

4 Paint the dark recess of the fireplace in permanent violet and the shaded side of the dresser in raw umber. Sketch the outline of the bowl of fruit on the table in yellow ochre and block in the oranges and bananas in the same colour, leaving the highlights untouched. Paint the reddest part of the apples in vermillion and begin putting in the red flowers on the curtains.

5 Paint the chair in vermillion. Although you are simply blocking in the underlying colour at this stage, without putting in any detailing, it will act as a glaze and establish the warm colour of the wood. At this point the artist decided to include another chair in his composition. He painted it in permanent violet as a chair in this position would be in shade and hence darker in tone than the other chair.

▶

6 Outline the stone jar on the hearth in the green mixture from Step 2. Begin putting in some of the detail of the painting on the wall. Paint the shadow under the fruit bowl in raw umber. Paint the tiled floor and the shaded sides of the table in magenta. Draw the outlines of two stemmed wine glasses on the table in green.

7 Glaze yellow ochre over the stone jar on the hearth. Paint the shaded sides of the chair in a dark, almost black mixture of red and green, leaving the seat red; immediately it begins to look more rounded and three-dimensional.

8 Outline a round bowl on the hearth in titanium white and block it in using yellow ochre. Paint the highlights on the stone jar in titanium white. Brush dilute titanium white over the tiled floor and the fireplace lintel. Use a thicker mix of titanium white to paint the checks on the tablecloth. Brush ultramarine blue over the fireplace recess and the shaded side of the dresser. Leave to dry.

9 Using the tip of your painting knife, scratch off paint in the shape of the outline of the candle sconce in the fireplace. Still using the painting knife, scratch off paint to create highlights on the back of the chair. You could equally well paint these elements in white, but sgraffito imparts a lively quality to the work and is an interesting technique to experiment with.

10 Paint the lines of the bricks in vermillion. Mix a dull brown from raw umber and cadmium yellow light and paint the picture frame. Glaze the same colour over the shaded side of the dresser, which you painted blue in Step 8.

Tip: Because the colours in glazes mix optically, rather than physically, the mixes often look more lively.

Assessment time
The overall warm mood of the scene has been set. Although the colours may look unnatural at this stage, they will be modified as the painting progresses. Never be afraid to alter things halfway through if you feel they're not working. At this point the artist decided that the checked tablecloth was overpowering the image and that the chair-back in the immediate foreground blocked the viewer's eye from moving through the picture. Radical changes were needed!

The rich, warm colours look very dominant at this stage, but they provide a warm undertone for the scene.

The chair-back interferes with the composition.

11 Using a large flat wash brush, brush titanium white over the tablecloth and the tiled floor, carefully brushing around the stone jar on the hearth and between the struts on the chair. At this point the artist also painted out the chair in the immediate foreground, which he felt had become too intrusive, and at the same time added another chair-back to the fireplace end of the table.

12 Complete the pattern on the curtains using cerulean blue and cadmium red. Using a small round brush, paint the china in the dresser in cerulean blue. Mix a mid-toned brown from cadmium yellow light, raw umber and titanium white and brush this mixture over the dresser. The colour now looks more natural, but it still retains the warm glow of the underlying orange.

▶

13 Finish painting the china in the dresser. As it is behind glass, which reflects the light, it is hard to see any detail in the china, so a general impression of the shapes will suffice.

14 Using a small brush, brush thin diagonal strokes of dilute titanium white and white mixed with cerulean blue over the glass doors in the dresser to show how the glass reflects light from the window.

15 Glaze the floor with a mixture of vermillion and titanium white. Paint white highlights on the fruit.

 Tip: Allow some of the previous white to show through on the floor, as this creates the impression of light being reflected off the glazed tiles.

16 Use the mid-toned brown mixture from Step 12 to give the chairs their natural wood colour, leaving the previous purplish tone visible in the most deeply shaded parts. Adjust the tones on the fruits so that they look rounded, using the same colours as before. The bananas, in particular, look too light so paint them again in cadmium yellow deep using permanent violet for the shaded facets.

The finished painting

This is a colourful, contemporary-looking painting. The composition looks informal but has been carefully considered, while the choice of predominantly warm colours creates a cosy and inviting mood. The flowers and fruit contrast well with the solidity of the furniture and fireplace and provide a homely touch that tells us this is a domestic interior.

The colour is built up in glazes, creating the effect of light shining on the tiled floor.

The flowers are loosely painted and enliven the composition.

The underlying colours modify subsequent glazes and help to create the wood texture.

Painting people

People are one of the most challenging and rewarding of all subjects to paint and your aim should be to capture not only a good likeness but also something of the sitter's character and personality.

Whether you're painting a head-and-shoulders portrait or a full-length study, it's generally advisable to start by making a reasonably detailed underdrawing. Take careful measurements and concentrate, in particular, on establishing the position of the facial features.

One of the joys of using oils or acrylics for painting people is the ease with which you can blend colours wet into wet on the support, to create almost imperceptible transitions from one tone to another. This is invaluable when painting flesh tones: the contours of the body are generally soft and rounded, which means that differences in tone can be very subtle – but they are critical in achieving a sense of light and shade and making your subject look three-dimensional. The same technique can be used for painting hair.

If you are new to portrait painting, start with a simple set-up – a plain background and perhaps just one light positioned to one side of your model to cast an obvious shadow. A head-on view, with the model looking directly at you, is the best way to begin. With a profile there are other complications to bear in mind, such as how the nose breaks the line of the cheek.

As you gain more experience and confidence, you can begin to introduce more elements – props that tell us something about the sitter's interests, a domestic interior that reveals something of their lifestyle, even a street scene of people going about their everyday business. Take care not to overcomplicate things, however, or the background will begin to detract from the portrait.

Venice grainseller ▼
In the contre-jour scene such as this, with the light coming from behind the subject, detail is subdued. Nonetheless, the shapes and overall proportions must look right.

Down to the sea ▲
We cannot see the faces in this delightful painting of a mother and her children walking towards the sea, which imparts a somewhat enigmatic mood to the scene, inviting us to make up our own story about who they are and what they are doing.

Brittany market ▶
The figures are almost incidental to this colourful market scene, as we can see very little of the facial detail, but the stances have been carefully observed and they bring life to the scene.

Tips: Whatever medium you are using, begin with thin applications of paint.
- Treat a portrait in the same way as you would any other subject: plot the facial features systematically, and a likeness will follow.
- Pay attention to things like spectacles and clothes that will give a clue as to what the person is like.
- Assess skin tones carefully. The transitions between one tone and another are subtle, but they help to establish the different planes of the body.

Portrait of a young child

There are several things to remember when you are drawing or painting a portrait of a child. The first is that young children are very active and have a short attention span: you cannot realistically expect them to sit still for hours while you work on your portrait, and for this reason you will probably find it easiest to work from a photograph.

Second, in children the head is much larger in relation to the overall body size than it is in adults. Although the human race is infinitely varied, as a general guide-line the head is about one-seventh of the total height of the body in adults – but in babies it may occupy almost as much as one-third of the total. The little girl in this portrait is about two years old: her head represents approximately one-quarter of her total height.

This project starts by toning the sup-port – a classic technique that was much used by some of the great portraitists such as Peter Paul Rubens (1577–1640). This provides the advantage of starting to paint from a mid-tone background, rather than a stark white ground, which makes it easier to judge the subtle flesh tones and the effects of light and shade cast by the sun. It also establishes the overall colour temperature of the portrait from the outset. In this instance, burnt sienna gives the portrait a lovely warm glow, which is particularly appropriate to the dappled sunlight that illuminates the scene.

Materials
- *Board primed with acrylic gesso*
- *Acrylic paints: burnt sienna, ultramarine blue, titanium white, cadmium red, lemon yellow, alizarin crimson, phthalocyanine green*
- *Brushes: small round, medium flat, small flat*
- *Rag*
- *Matt acrylic medium*

The pose
Relaxed and informal, this child's attention is occupied by something that we cannot see. Note that she is positioned slightly off centre. If a figure in a portrait is looking off to one side, it is generally better to have more space on that side, as this creates a calmer, more restful mood. Placing a figure close to the edge of the frame creates a feeling of tension.

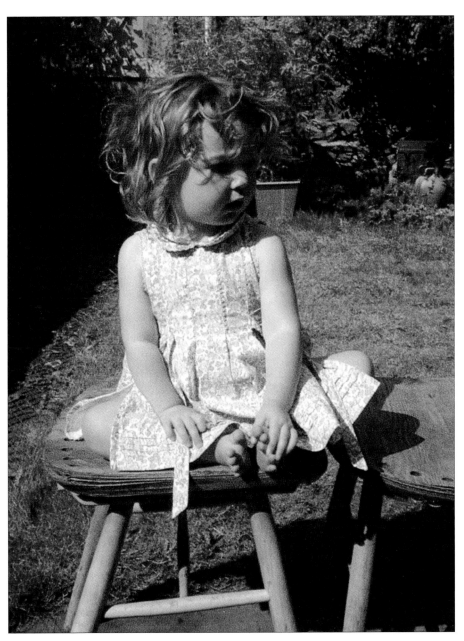

Preliminary sketch
Flesh tones can be tricky, and you may find it useful to make a quick colour sketch experimenting with different mixes, such as the one shown on the left, before you start painting.

1 Tone the primed board with burnt sienna acrylic paint and leave to dry. Mix a dilute, warm brown from burnt sienna and a little ultramarine blue. Using a small round brush, make a loose underdrawing, concentrating on getting the overall proportions and the angles of the head and limbs correct.

2 Mix a darker, less dilute brown, this time using more ultramarine blue. Using the small round brush, put in the darkest tones of the hair, the shadows on the face and under the collar of the girl's dress, and the main creases in the fabric of the dress. These creases help to convey form.

3 Mix a very pale pink from titanium white, cadmium red and a little lemon yellow and paint the palest flesh tones on the face, arms and legs, as well as some highlights in the hair. Add more water and put in the lightest tones of the girl's dress. Note how the colour of the support shows through.

4 Mix a warm purple from ultramarine blue and alizarin crimson. Using a medium flat brush, block in the dark foliage area to the left of the girl. Add more water and ultramarine blue to the mixture and paint the darkest foliage areas to the right of the girl and the shadows under the stool.

▶

5 Mix a bright green from phthalocyanine green, lemon yellow, titanium white and a little cadmium red. Block in the lawn and background foliage. Use less lemon yellow for the shaded grass and more white for the brightest parts.

6 Mix a very pale green from titanium white and phthalocyanine green and brush it loosely over the child's sun-bleached cotton dress.

7 Mix a dark brown from burnt sienna and ultramarine blue and start to put some detailing in the hair and on the shadowed side of the face. Mix a warm shadow tone from alizarin crimson and burnt sienna and build up the shadow tones on the left-hand (sunlit) side of the face, alternating between this mixture and the pale pink used in Step 3.

8 Add titanium white to the purple mixture from Step 4 and paint the stool to the right of the child. Paint the stool on which she is sitting in a mixture of brown and titanium white, with brushstrokes that follow the wood grain. Mix a rich brown from burnt sienna and alizarin crimson and, using a small round brush, paint the shadows at the bottom of her dress.

9 Dab some of the purple mixture (the stool colour) over the background foliage. Using the same colour in this area establishes a visual link between foreground and background; the light colour also creates the impression of dappled light in the foliage. Mix a dark, bluish green from ultramarine blue and phthalocyanine green and paint the shadow under the dress collar and any deep creases and shadows in the fabric of the dress.

10 Using the pale pink mixture from Step 3 and a round brush, go over the arms and legs again, carefully blending the tones wet into wet on the support in order to convey the roundness of the flesh.

Assessment time
The blocks of colour are now taking on some meaning and form: for the rest of the painting, concentrate on building up the form and detailing.

The tonal contrasts on the face are too extreme and need to be blended to make the skin look more life-like.

The hands and feet, in particular, need to be given more definition.

The child is not sufficiently well separated from the background.

Tip: To make flesh look soft and rounded, you need to blend the tones on the support so that they merge almost imperceptibly; it is rare to see a sharp transition from one tone to another. Working wet into wet is the best way to achieve this, gradually darkening the tone as the limb turns away from the light. With acrylic paints, you may find that adding a few drops of flow improver helps matters: flow improver increases the flow of the paint and its absorption into the support surface.

11 Mix burnt sienna with a tiny amount of titanium white. Using a small round brush, paint the dark spaces between the fingers and the shadows between the feet and on the toes. Try to see complicated areas such as these as abstract shapes and blocks of colour: if you start thinking of them as individual toes, the chances are that you will make them bigger than they should be.

12 Refine the facial details, using the same mixes as before. Put in the curve of the ear, which is just visible through the hair, using the pale pink skin tone. Mix a reddish brown from alizarin crimson, ultramarine blue and burnt sienna. Build up the volume of the hair, looking at the general direction of the hair growth and painting clumps rather than individual hairs.

13 Using the purple shadow mixture from Step 4 and a small flat brush, cut in around the head to define the edge and provide better separation between the girl and the background. Mix a dark green from phthalocyanine green and ultramarine blue and loosely dab it over the dark foliage area to provide more texture. Using cool colours here makes this area recede, focusing attention on the little girl.

14 Add a little matt acrylic medium to the pale pink flesh tone and go over the light areas of the face, working the paint in with the brush so that it blends well and covers any areas that are too dark in tone. The matt medium makes the paint more translucent, so that it is more like a glaze. Do the same thing on the arms, adding a little burnt sienna for any areas that are slightly warmer in tone.

15 Make any final adjustments that you deem necessary. Here, the artist felt that the girl's hands were too small, making her look slightly doll-like; using the pale flesh colour from previous steps, she carefully painted over them to make them a little broader and bring them up to the right scale.

The finished painting

This is a charming portrait of a toddler with her slightly chubby face and arms, rounded mouth, big eyes, and unselfconscious pose. There is just enough detail in the background to establish the outdoor setting, but by paying very careful attention to the tones of the highlights and shadows, the artist has captured the dappled sunlight that pervades the scene.

Although no detail is visible in the eyes, we are nonetheless invited to follow the child's gaze.

Subtle blending of colour on the child's arms and face makes the flesh look soft and rounded.

There is just enough background to give the scene a context without distracting from the portrait.

Brushstrokes on the stool follow the direction of the woodgrain – an effective way of conveying both pattern and texture.

Head-and-shoulders portrait

The surroundings and clothing in this head-and-shoulders portrait have been kept deliberately simple in order to give you an opportunity to practise painting skin tones.

You might think it would make life very simple for artists if there was a ready-mixed skin colour that could be used in all circumstances. However, although you may come across a so-called "flesh tone" in some paint manufacturers' catalogues, it cannot cope with the sheer variety of skin tones that you are likely to encounter.

Even in models with the most flawless of complexions, the skin will not be a uniform colour in all areas. The actual colour (particularly in fair-skinned individuals) can vary dramatically from one part of the subject to another: the cheeks, for example, often look redder than the forehead or chin simply because the blood vessels are closer to the surface. And, just as with any other subject, you need to use different tones in order to make your subject look three-dimensional. To understand this, look at black-and-white magazine photographs of models with good bone structure: note how the cheekbones cast a shadow on the lower part of the face. Even though (thanks to make-up) the skin colour may be virtually the same all over the face, in strong lighting there may be big differences in tone.

You also need to think about colour temperature: using cool colours for the shadows and warmer ones for the lit areas is a good way of showing how the light falls on your model. Although cool blues and purples might seem strange colours to use for painting skin, it is surprising how using them with warmer colours can bring a portrait to life.

The same principles of colour temperature also apply to the light that illuminates your subject. Although we are generally unaware of the differences, the colour of sunlight is not as warm as, say, artificial tungsten lighting. It's hard to be precise about the colours you should use for painting skin tones, as the permutations are almost infinite, so the best advice is simply to paint what you can actually observe rather than what you think is the right colour.

Materials
- *Board primed with acrylic gesso*
- *B pencil*
- *Acrylic paints: Turner's yellow, cadmium red, titanium white, burnt umber, cadmium yellow, lamp black, phthalocyanine blue, alizarin crimson, yellow ochre*
- *Brushes: large flat, medium flat, small flat*

The pose
A three-quarters pose with the light coming from one side, as here, is generally more interesting to paint than a head-on pose, as it allows you to have one side of the face in shadow, thus creating modelling on the facial features. The lighting also creates highlights in the model's dark eyes, which always helps to bring a portrait to life. Although this model was sitting in front of a very busy background, the artist chose to simplify it to a uniform background colour in the finished portrait to avoid drawing attention away from the face.

1 Using a B pencil, lightly sketch your subject, indicating the fall of the hair, the facial features and the areas of shadow. Put in as much detail as you wish; it is particularly important to get the size and position of the facial features right.

2 Mix a light flesh tone from Turner's yellow, cadmium red and titanium white. Using a medium flat brush, block in the face and neck, adding a little burnt umber for the shadowed side of the face.

3 Add a little more cadmium red to the flesh-tone mixture and use it to darken the tones on the shadowed side of the face, under the chin and on the neck. Mix a red-biased orangey mix from cadmium red and cadmium yellow and paint the cheek and the shadowed side of the neck and the shaded area that lies immediately under the mouth. Immediately the portrait is taking on a feeling of light and shade.

4 Mix a pale bluish black from lamp black and phthalocyanine blue and begin putting in the lightest tones of the hair, making sure your brushstrokes follow the direction in which the hair grows. When the first tone is dry, add burnt umber to the mixture and paint the darker areas within the hair mass to give the hair volume. Add more phthalocyanine blue to the mixture and paint the model's shirt.

▶

5 Mix a pale brown from cadmium red, burnt umber, Turner's yellow and titanium white and loosely block in the background, painting carefully around the face. You may find it easier to switch to a larger brush for this stage, as it will allow you to cover a wide area more quickly.

6 Mix a rich, dark brown from lamp black, burnt umber, cadmium red and a little of the blue shirt mixture. Using a small flat brush, paint the dark of the eyes and the lashes, taking care to get the shape of the white of the eye right. Use the same colour for the nostril.

7 Use the same colour to define the line between the upper and lower lips. Mix a reddish brown from burnt umber and phthalocyanine blue and paint the shadows under the eyes and inside the eye sockets.

8 Paint the mouth in varying mixes of alizarin crimson, cadmium red and yellow ochre, leaving the highlights untouched. The highlights will be worked into later, using lighter colours.

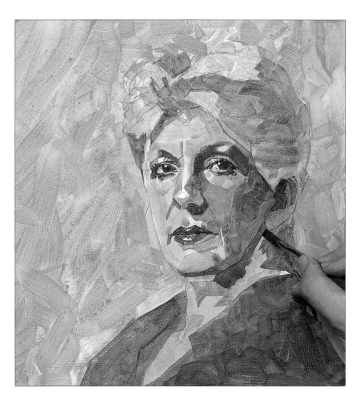

9 Darken the flesh tones on the shaded side of the face where necessary, using a mixture of alizarin crimson, phthalocyanine blue and a little titanium white, adding more blue to the mixture for the shadow under the chin, which is cooler in tone.

10 Mix a dark but warm black from burnt umber and lamp black and paint the darkest sections of the hair, leaving the lightest colour (applied in Step 4) showing through in places. This gives tonal variety and shows how the light falls on the hair.

11 Add more water to the mixture to make it more dilute and go over the dark areas of the hair again, this time leaving only a few highlights showing through as relatively fine lines.

12 Mix a dark blue from phthalocyanine blue and lamp black and paint over the shirt again, leaving some of the lighter blue areas applied in Step 4 showing through. Your brushstrokes should follow the direction and fall of the fabric.

▶

13 The beauty of acrylics is that you can paint a light colour over a dark one, without the first colour being visible. If you think the background is too dark and there is not sufficient differentiation between the model and the background, mix a warm off-white from titanium white, yellow ochre and burnt umber and, using a large flat brush, loosely paint the background again.

14 Using a small flat brush, cut around individual hairs with the background colour, carefully looking at the "negative shapes".

15 Using a fine round brush and titanium white straight from the tube, dot the highlights on to the eyes, nose and lower lip.

The finished painting

This is a relatively simple portrait, with nothing to distract from the sitter's direct gaze. Although the colour palette is limited, the artist has achieved an impressive and realistic range of skin and hair tones. Interest comes from the use of semi-transparent paint layers and allowing the directions of the brush marks to show through.

Carefully positioned highlights in the eyes make them sparkle and bring the portrait to life.

Variations in the skin tone, particularly on the shaded side of the face, help to reveal the shape of the face and its underlying bone structure.

The highlights in the hair are created by putting down the lightest tones first and allowing them to show through subsequent applications of paint.

Café scene

At first glance, this café and street scene looks extremely complicated and full of movement, with a complex play of light and shade across the whole scene. You could be forgiven for wondering how on earth you can capture such a wealth of detail in paint.

The trick, at least in the initial stages, is to forget about the detail and to concentrate instead on the overall impression. Look for blocks of colour and tone – and try to see the scene as a series of interconnecting shapes, rather than as individual elements. If you get too caught up in details such as a person's hair or the precise pattern on one of the café umbrellas, the chances are that your painting will become tight and laboured.

Remember, too, that the spaces between objects (which artists describe as "negative" shapes) are as important in a painting as the objects themselves (the "positive" shapes). Although the rational part of your brain may be telling you that a person or a solid object such as a table should take precedence over an apparently empty background, in painting terms the two are equally important: one helps to define the other.

The complex pattern of light and shade requires careful treatment, too. There are many shadows here, both in the open foreground and in the dark, narrow street in the background. Shadows are rarely, if ever, black; instead, they often contain colours that are complementary to the main subject. If buildings are a warm terracotta colour, for example, their shadows may contain a little complementary green.

Sketch
Scenes of people can change quickly, so make a quick preliminary sketch to capture the moment.

Materials
- *Board primed with acrylic gesso*
- *Willow charcoal*
- *Acrylic paints: cadmium yellow, cadmium red, titanium white, phthalocyanine green, alizarin crimson, lemon yellow, ultramarine blue*
- *Brushes: large round, medium flat, small round*
- *Absorbent paper towel*

The scene
This is one type of subject in which painting from photographs really comes into its own. There is so much going on that you could do little more than put down the bare bones of the scene on the spot – but a quick reference photo or two will "freeze" the action and provide you with plenty of information on which to base your image.

1 Block in the darkest areas of the background buildings and the shadows on the pavement, using the side of a stick of willow charcoal, as this allows you to cover large areas quickly. Although the charcoal will be covered up by subsequent applications of paint, it allows you to establish the structure of the scene at the outset, and makes it easier for you to find your way around the complex mix of colours and tones.

2 To avoid dirtying your colours when you begin applying the paint, gently dust off any excess charcoal powder using a clean piece of paper towel. (Alternatively, you could use a spray fixative.)

3 Mix a warm orange from cadmium yellow and cadmium red. Using a large round brush, brush in the warm colours of background buildings. Paint the café umbrellas and awning in mixtures of cadmium red and titanium white, varying the proportions of the two colours to get the right tones. Putting in these strong tones in the early stages helps give the scene some structure. The order in which you apply them is not terribly important, but while you have got one colour on the palette try to use it everywhere that it occurs.

4 Loosely indicate the café tables in phthalocyanine green. Mix a very dilute green from phthalocyanine green and titanium white and paint the shadow areas in the foreground. (Note that this green is a cool complementary colour to the reds used on the awning and umbrellas.) Add alizarin crimson to the mixture and paint the very dark colours of the buildings in the background. This gives you the necessary darkness of tone without having to resort to using black, which often tends to look flat and lifeless. It also picks up on colours used elsewhere in the painting, creating one of many colour links that will ultimately help to hold the whole image together.

▶

5 Mix a pale yellow from lemon yellow and titanium white and put in the light-coloured buildings in the background. Add more titanium white to the mixtures that you used to paint the umbrellas in Step 3, making the paint fairly thick, and paint the pinkish stripes on the umbrellas.

6 Using the dark mixture from Step 4, begin blocking in the figures sitting at the café tables. Do not try to put in substantial detail at this stage: simply look for the overall shapes. Look at the tilt of people's shoulders and heads and concentrate on getting these angles right, as they will help to make the painting look realistic. Brush more of the dilute phthalocyanine green and white mixture over the street area, particularly at the point just beyond the café where the street narrows and is in deeper shade.

7 Block in the colours of the shirts of the café customers in the foreground, making the colours darker in tone for the creases in the fabric, as this helps to reveal the form of the body and give more of a sense of light and shade.

8 Brush over the highlight areas with titanium white, using the paint thickly in order to create some texture. Deepen the tones of the big foreground umbrella where necessary. Using the same dark mixtures as before, carefully brush around the figures sitting at the café tables; although the figures are little more than blocks of colour at this stage, and very little detail has been put in, defining the negative shapes (the spaces between the figures) in this way helps to separate them from the background so that they stand out more clearly.

Assessment time

Using brilliant blue and alizarin crimson, block in more of the shirt and trouser colours of the passers-by on the left. The main elements are now in place, and the rest of the painting will be a gradual process of refinement: although they may look like fairly abstract blocks of colour at this stage, the subjects will soon start to emerge more clearly. Training yourself to look for blocks of colour, rather than attempting to define every element, is a useful exercise.

The dark blocks laid down in Step 1 provide the structure for the image.

The people are painted as bold blocks of colour; detail can be added later once the basic shapes and colours are in place.

9 Pick out details using a small round brush. Paint the curved chair backs in phthalocyanine green, and the hair of the café customers in various browns mixed from cadmium yellow and cadmium red. Remember to look carefully at the spaces between objects as well as at the objects themselves: going around the figures in a dark tone helps to make them stand out.

10 Continue adding defining details across the painting, again looking at the negative spaces and looking for identifiable blocks of colour on the clothes of the passers-by. Vertical strokes of green on the background buildings are a quick-and-easy way of implying the dark window recesses; the colour also provides a visual link with the green chairs in the foreground.

11 Because it is so bright, the eye is drawn to the paved foreground area in the bottom left of the painting, which looks very empty. Using more of the green mixture from Step 6 and a medium flat brush, make broad horizontal strokes across this area. This enhances the feeling of dappled light playing on the ground and creates texture and interest.

12 Switching to a medium flat brush allows you to shape straight-edged elements, such as the eaves of the roofs (top right) and the table edges (bottom right), more precisely.

13 Using a pale, blue-grey mixture of titanium white and ultramarine blue, loosely indicate the lettering on the café awning. Continue adjusting tones across the whole scene: adding a pale, but opaque yellow to the background buildings reinforces the sense of light and shade, while the shadows on the ground can be made stronger with a bluish-purple mixture as before.

14 Using the flat brush again, block in rectangles of colour on the roofs to define their edges more clearly. The precise colours that you use are not too important: look for the relative lightness and darkness of different areas, as this is what will make the picture look three-dimensional.

15 Using a fine round brush and the same pale blue-grey mixture that you used for the café awning lettering, "draw" in the vertical posts of the awning and the large foreground umbrellas. Adjust the tones on the shaded sides of both awning and umbrellas, if necessary, to reinforce the different planes of the image. If you decide that the bottom left corner is still too bright in relation to the rest of the painting, brush more of the bluey-green shadow mixture across it. Finally, look for any areas that catch the light, such as the edges of the foreground tables and chairs, and lightly touch in the highlights here with a pale mixture of phthalocyanine green and titanium white.

The finished painting

This is a spontaneous-looking painting that belies its careful planning and the meticulous attention to capturing the effects of light and shade. The composition looks informal, like a snapshot of a moment "frozen" in time; in fact, the large, virtually empty space on the left helps to balance the image, while the receding lines of the café tables lead the viewer's eye through the picture to the bustling street and buildings in the background.

Creating the right tonal balance is one of the keys to an image like this; resisting the temptation to put in too much detail, with the consequent risk of overworking the painting, is another. Here, the artist has succeeded on both counts.

Deep shadows reveal the intensity of the sunlight. They are balanced by the large, brightly lit buildings in the background and help to bring the scene to life.

Although there is relatively little detail on the faces, by concentrating on the tilt of the heads and bodies the artist has conveyed a feeling of animation.

The artist has used some artistic licence in choosing the colours for the building in the background, but they complement and balance the foreground colours well.

Reclining nude

The reclining nude – more particularly, the reclining female nude – is a classic subject in Western art.

There are a few practical considerations to take into account – particularly if you are painting from life. First, make sure your model is comfortable: provide a sofa, blanket or other soft surface for her to lie on and make sure that the room is warm and free of draughts.

As far as the pose is concerned, it is often better to allow the model to settle into a position that feels natural to her than to tell her what pose to adopt. Although you can obtain interesting and dynamic paintings by directing the model to tense her muscles, such poses are difficult to hold for any length of time.

This particular pose is easy to hold, even for a relatively long period of time. The model's weight is evenly distributed along the whole length of her body and she is able to rest her head on her right forearm, cupping her hand around her head for extra support.

The differences in flesh tone need to be very carefully assessed in this project. Certain areas, such as the hands, the soles of the feet and the lower body, tend to be warmer in colour than others, because the blood vessels run closer to the surface of the skin. The upper body, on the other hand, is usually cooler in tone. However, one of the joys of painting in oils is that the paint remains soft and workable for a long time, so you can blend colours on the support as you work to create subtle transitions from one tone to another as the body curves towards or away from the light source.

Materials
- *Stretched canvas*
- *Rag*
- *Oil paints: cadmium orange, brilliant pink, raw sienna, cadmium red, cadmium yellow, brilliant turquoise, titanium white, ultramarine blue, lamp black, vermilion, cerulean blue*
- *Turpentine (white spirit)*
- *Drying linseed oil*
- *Brushes: selection of small and medium rounds, small or medium flat*

The pose
One of the most interesting things about this particular model is the way in which her upper vertebrae and ribs are so clearly defined. The natural curves of her body create clearly defined areas of light and shade, which add interest to the composition. Note the masking tape on the blanket, outlining the model's pose. This enables the model to get back in the same position if she inadvertently moves during the session or has to take a break.

1 With a rag, spread cadmium orange paint evenly over the canvas, changing to brilliant pink in the top left. Leave to dry.

2 Using a medium round brush and raw sienna, "draw" the edges of the blanket on which the model is lying and the dark shadow under her hips. Delineate the head and upper body and the legs in cadmium red. The actual colours are not too important at this stage, as this is merely the underpainting, but warm colours are appropriate to the subject. Mix a range of warm flesh tones from cadmium yellow and cadmium orange and block in the warmest toned areas – the buttocks, the soles of the feet, and the curve of the spine. Start putting in the main folds of the background cloth using mixtures of brilliant turquoise and titanium white.

3 Mix titanium white with a little ultramarine blue and block in some of the dark folds in the background cloth. Using a fine brush and cadmium red, loosely "draw" the head and supporting hand, reinforce the line separating the legs and indicate the angle of the hips.

> **Tip:** It is always important to remember the underlying anatomy of the pose, even when you are painting fleshy parts of the body where the shape of the bones is not visible.

4 Using green (mixed from titanium white, cadmium yellow and ultramarine blue) and a dark grey (mixed from ultramarine blue and raw sienna), start putting in the pattern of the patchwork blanket. Mix a pale blue-green from ultramarine blue and raw sienna and indicate the shadows under the ribs and the shaded part of the back. Note that this mixture is a complementary colour to the first flesh tones: shadow areas often contain a hint of a complementary colour.

5 Mix a pale orange from cadmium red, cadmium yellow and titanium white and begin putting in some of the paler flesh tones. Alternate between all the various flesh tones on your palette, blending them into one another on the support and continually assessing where the light and dark tones fall and whether the colours are warm or cool in temperature. Almost immediately, you will see that the body is starting to look three-dimensional.

6 Continue working on the flesh tones. The highlights and shadows reveal the curves of the body: the backs of the thighs, for example, are in shadow and are therefore darker in tone than the tops of the buttocks, which are angled towards the light. Note the greenish tones on the upper body: the upper body is often noticeably cooler in tone than the lower body, perhaps because the blood vessels in this area are not so near the surface of the skin.

7 Block in the most deeply shaded areas of the white background cloth with a blue-biased mixture of ultramarine blue and titanium white. Use a slightly lighter version of this colour to paint the model's shaved head, allowing some of the ground to show through in parts as the colour of her scalp. Loosely "draw" the hand and fingers in cadmium red, indicating the joints in the fingers by means of rough circular or elliptical shapes.

Assessment time

Although the areas of warm and cool tone have been established, the figure still looks somewhat flat and two-dimensional. More tonal contrast is needed: spend time working out how you are going to achieve this. Remember to work across the picture as a whole rather than concentrating on one area – otherwise you run the risk of over-emphasizing certain areas and making them too detailed in relation to the rest, thus destroying the balance of the painting.

The broad areas of light and shade have been established – now you can refine this area.

There is not enough tonal contrast for the figure to look truly three-dimensional.

8 The cloth at the model's feet is draped to create interesting folds. Block in its shape loosely in a mixture of ultramarine blue and white, then put dark strokes of a darker grey or brown over the top to indicate the main folds. Begin putting in some of the mid-tones in the background cloth, using mixtures of ultramarine blue and white as before.

9 Loosely paint the pattern of the patchwork blanket on which the model is lying, using broad strokes of the appropriate colour. Do not try to be too precise with the pattern: a loose interpretation will suffice. You should, however, note how the lines of the pattern change direction where the blanket is not perfectly flat.

10 Continue working on the blanket, gradually building up and strengthening the colours while keeping them fresh and spontaneous.

11 Redefine the fingers in cadmium orange and a little brilliant pink.

12 Darken the area around the head with a mixture of ultramarine blue, white and a little lamp black, so that the head stands out from the background. Work on the flesh tones, to improve the tonal contrast: the shoulder blade, for example, is lighter than the tones laid down so far, so paint it in a mixture of cadmium orange and white. Use the same colour to define the highlights on the top cervical vertebrae. The soles of the feet are very warm in colour; paint them in a mixture of cadmium red and vermilion.

▶

13 Now turn your attention to the background cloth, reinforcing the dark and mid-toned folds with a mixture of ultramarine blue, white and a tiny amount of cerulean blue – all the time assessing the tones of the cloth in relation to the overall scene rather than looking at it in isolation.

14 Use pure white for the brightest areas of the background cloth, changing to a smaller brush for the finest creases. Note how the folds vary in tone depending on how deep they are: use some mid-tones where necessary to convey this.

15 Mix a dark green from ultramarine blue and cadmium yellow and reinforce the dark colours in the blanket. Use the same colour to strengthen the shadow under the model and give a sharp edge to the curve of her body. Brighten the light greens and pinks in the blanket; as the patchwork pattern is made up of straight strips of fabric, you may find that it helps to switch to a small or medium flat brush so that the lines of the pattern are straight and crisp-edged.

16 The triangular-shaped wedge of cloth on the right, just above the model's head, is too light and leads the viewer's eye out of the picture. Mix a mid-toned green and block it in, directing your brushstrokes upwards to avoid accidentally brushing paint on to the model's head.

The finished painting

The figure is positioned almost exactly across the centre of the picture – something that artists are often advised to avoid, but in this instance it adds to the calm, restful mood of the painting. The dark colours and sloping lines of the blanket and the folds in the background cloth all help to direct the viewer's eye towards the nude figure. The background cloth is painted slightly darker in tone than it is in reality: overly stark whites would detract from the figure.

The legs are slightly bent: light and dark flesh tones show how some parts are angled into the light while others are shaded.

Careful assessment of tones is required in order to paint the white backcloth convincingly.

Skin is stretched taut over the ribs and upper vertebrae: subtle shading reveals the shape of the underlying bones.

Cupped hands

Hands and gestures are very expressive and can tell you a lot about a person's character and mood. Sadly, many people seem to find it difficult to draw and paint hands – and the reason is usually that they give too much attention to individual elements such as the fingers, rather than trying to see the hand as a whole. You should always try to think of the hand as a complete unit rather than as something made up of four fingers and a thumb. If you paint each finger separately, the chances are that you'll make them too big in relation to the rest of the hand.

This project is a simple pose that gives you the chance to examine the structure of the hand in some detail.

Before you begin the painting, spend time looking your own hands. Some people's fingers are short and stubby, while others have long, elegantly tapering fingers; nonetheless, you will be able to make some general observations that apply to all hands. Look at the number of joints and see how the fingers widen slightly at these points. Spread your hand out flat: you will see that each finger is a different length and that the joints do not align with one another. Similarly, the knuckles run in a curved line across the back of the hand. Arch your hand, with your fingertips placed on the table top and your wrist elevated, so that you can see the bones and tendons that connect the fingers to the rest of the hand and arm.

Finally, note how the creases in the skin, and subtle changes in tone as each finger turns away from the light, will help you to create a three-dimensional impression.

Materials

- *B pencil*
- *Board primed with acrylic gesso*
- *Acrylic paints: raw umber, ultramarine blue, cadmium red, cadmium lemon, titanium white, quinacridone red*
- *Brushes: medium flat, small flat*

The pose

In this project the sitter's hands are clasped loosely around a cup of coffee – a pose that is easy for the sitter to hold, giving you plenty of time to make your study. The structure of the fingers and the way the joints are articulated can be seen clearly. Light comes from the top left of the scene and causes the cup to cast interestingly shaped shadows on the sitter's left hand.

1 Using a B pencil, make a light underdrawing. Mix a dark brown from raw umber and ultramarine blue and, using a flat brush, paint in the shadows above and below the fingers. Add a little cadmium red and block in the shadows on the sitter's left hand.

2 Mix in a little more red. Paint the shadow on the finger undersides.

3 Paint the hands in a mix of cadmium red, raw umber and cadmium lemon, and paint the coffee in a mix of raw umber and cadmium red. Mix grey from ultramarine and raw umber and paint the shaded parts of the mug. Lighten the mix and paint the rest of the mug.

4 Add a little more ultramarine blue to the mixture used for the coffee mug and paint the sitter's trousers. Paint the reddish brown area between the sitter's legs in a mixture of cadmium red and raw umber.

5 Mix cadmium red, raw umber, cadmium lemon and a little titanium white and paint the mid-pink tones on the hands. Note how the changes in tone between the different segments of the fingers define their form.

Assessment time
We are beginning to get some sense of the shape of the hands and how the fingers bend, but the tonal differences are not yet sufficient for them to look fully rounded. The

background and the hands are, at this stage, too similar in tone; as a result, the hands do not stand out clearly. Overall, the colours are too pale and need to be strengthened.

The form of the hands needs to be more fully developed.

The hands merge into the background.

▶

6 Mix a dark brown from raw umber and ultramarine blue and paint over the coffee again, adding a little white to the mixture for areas where the light hits the liquid. It is important to realize that the coffee is not a uniform shade of brown throughout.

7 Mix a neutral grey from ultramarine blue, raw umber and titanium white and put in the shadows on the trousers caused by creases and folds in the fabric. Darken the flesh tone overall, leaving little areas of light tone on the nails, which are shiny and catch the light.

8 Darken the brown between the legs. Immediately, the hands start to stand out from the background.

9 Use a range of dark neutral greys to paint the shadows cast on the mug by the fingers.

10 Using lighter tones of grey and white, tidy up the tones on the coffee mug.

11 Darken the background – the sitter's trousers. This throws the hands forward to become the main focus of the painting.

12 Lighten the flesh tones where necessary and refine the tones on the fingers, making use of the same mixtures as before.

13 Darken the shadows on the left hand using raw umber, quinacridone red and ultramarine blue. This gives depth to the scene.

The finished painting

This is a simple and relaxed pose that has been skilfully painted, with careful attention being paid to the different flesh tones in order to convey the shape of the hands and the way the fingers curl around the coffee mug. The background is a plain colour, which allows the hands (the focal point of the image) to stand out clearly.

Shadows cast by the fingers reveal both the direction and the intensity of the light.

The dark background allows the hands to stand out clearly.

Changes in tone, delineated with a flat brush, reveal the form of the fingers.

Index